Ollie Baines is the co-founde
that exists to share the gosp
from Canterbury Christ Church University with a degree in Physical
Education and Sport and Exercise Science in 2014. After graduating,
he pursued the avenue of sports journalism after earning an internship
with HITC Sport during the 2014 FIFA World Cup. Ollie then had
opportunities to write for Sky Sports and *Shoot* magazine, which in
turn led to a period as a freelance sports writer. He has since found
himself back in the education sector, working with special-needs
children. Ollie has recently been named in Premier Christian Radio's
feature article on 33 young Christian leaders for his work with Cross
The Line. A finalist of the 2015 Football Blogging Awards, Ollie is keen
to share the gospel message through his greatest passion, sport.

Liam Flint is the co-founder of Cross The Line and a finalist of the
2015 Football Blogging Awards. A graduate from Oxford Brookes
University in Physical Education and Sports Coaching, Liam lives
and breathes sport while working as a teaching assistant in primary
education. He is a keen writer, interviewer and people person. Most
importantly, he is a follower of Christ, and seeks to combine this
passion with sport, to reach many for the gospel.

CROSS THE LINE

*Christian footballers talk God,
faith and the beautiful game*

Ollie Baines and Liam Flint

First published in Great Britain in 2016

Society for Promoting Christian Knowledge
36 Causton Street
London SW1P 4ST
www.spck.org.uk

British Library Cataloguing-in-Publication Data
A catalogue record for this book is available from the British Library

ISBN 978-0-281-07680-2
eBook ISBN 978-0-281-07681-9

Typeset by Graphicraft Limited, Hong Kong
First printed in Great Britain by Ashford Colour Press
Subsequently digitally printed in Great Britain

eBook by Graphicraft Limited, Hong Kong

Produced on paper from sustainable forests

For God, who gave us the passion
and heart for Cross The Line.
We are merely his stewards carrying
out his work.

'For I am not ashamed of the gospel,
because it is the power of God that brings
salvation to everyone who believes.'
(Romans 1.16)

Contents

Acknowledgements

Players
We would like to say a massive thank you to the twenty footballers who so kindly gave us their time and were so open with us about their personal walks with God. Safe to say, without them there wouldn't be any substance for a book and we really appreciate their co-operation.

Clubs
Next we would like to sound our appreciation to the clubs and especially the media departments. They fielded our requests with grace and were so helpful. We understand that they are inundated with requests and we are truly thankful that they saw our inquiries and potential book as good value.

Agencies
We would also like to extend our gratitude towards player agencies. While all of the clubs gave their permission for our interviews to be published, we had the pleasure of liaising with several agencies and they were very co-operative in allowing us to speak with their clients.

SPCK
Of course, behind this book is a team of publishers. SPCK approached us in October 2015 and soon caught us up in their exciting vision for sharing the Christian faith through a book. When we heard about their proposal we immediately climbed on board and have thoroughly enjoyed working alongside Philip Law, Juliet Trickey, Olivia Carson, Neil Whyte and Dr Rima Devereaux. We will always be indebted to their passion and dedication to seeing our book come to fruition.

Special mentions

Behind the scenes there have been many invaluable connections that God has gifted us with. One of these is someone to whom we would like to offer our sincere thanks: Andy Searles, who is the volunteer chaplain at Orlando City soccer club. He has been instrumental in helping us to reach out to various chaplains and playing staff. His wealth of knowledge and experience has given us such a platform, on and off the field. We are excited to work with him in the future.

We would also like to express our gratitude to Jason Greenwich of Atleti di Cristo. Based in Milan, Jason has provided us with several exceptional player links that you can view in the book itself. He has been an advocate of Cross The Line and has always been keen to support us by any means possible.

We would like publicly to thank Premier Christian Radio, who have given us a significant platform to speak about the book – their continued support means a lot to us.

A massive thanks to our respective churches, Frinton Free Church and City Church Canterbury, who have immersed us in prayer and encouragement.

Thank you to our families, who have supported us financially and spiritually through all the highs and lows. They have always been there for us to offer advice and to stand with us in everything we do.

To our friends and house groups who have gone through each step and season with us; their prayers and support have helped us to make some big decisions that have ultimately led us to this point.

Finally and most importantly, we extend our gratitude, love and praise to God, the one who made this all possible and through whom we can do all things. From day one this has been his vision and we have been blessed to share in this with him.

Introduction

What is Cross The Line?

Cross The Line is an organization that exists to share the gospel through football. Since December 2014 we have been producing online football content on our website, <www.xtheline.co.uk>, sharing the good news of Jesus Christ to millions of readers across the globe.

About the authors

Ollie Baines and Liam Flint are the co-founders of Cross The Line, who both share a passion for football and their Christian faith.

What's our vision?

Our vision is to spread the gospel message and ultimately glorify God through our articles, player interviews, podcasts, testimonies and recent book. We believe that faith and football can go hand in hand to form a powerful synergy that can change lives.

Why write a book?

First, there is no book quite like this one out there for people to read. As football fans ourselves, we wanted to inspire and encourage people to see the beautiful game painted in a different light. This book is the perfect opportunity to show that there is so much more to these footballers than just what you see on the pitch.

How can you get involved?

In these exciting times at Cross The Line, we are always looking to expand our team. If you possess skills in writing, broadcasting, media or just have a passion for our vision, then we would love to hear from you.

Website – www.xtheline.co.uk
Email – crosstheline321@gmail.com
Twitter – @crossthelinex_
Facebook – Cross The Line
Instagram – crossthe_line

We hope you are left inspired by this book.

CROSS THE LINE

'My God is able'

Full name: **Odion Jude Ighalo**
DOB: 16 June 1989
Born: Lagos, Nigeria
Clubs: Prime, Julius Berger, Lyn, Udinese, Granada, Cesena, Watford
Position: Striker

Odion Ighalo

You've been in England for a little while now. What have you made of it so far?
Yeah, it has been great, England is known for its football and it's one of the best countries to play in the world. Also, playing in the Premier League is something I've always dreamt of and I am happy to be a part of it. I thank God for giving me the opportunity to play in it, so I'm very happy.

What made you sign for Watford?
Well, before I joined on loan I had been following the team for about two years when the Pozzo family took over Udinese. I thought it was a good team who could gain promotion to the Premier League one day. I felt I could help the team and fight together as one to get promoted. My aim was not to come and play Championship football for ever, it was to come and help the team get promoted to the Premier League, which I am very happy we have done.

You've already shown your goal-scoring capabilities. What's it like to score in the Premier League?
It's a great feeling for me, it's a great moment because as a striker you want to score goals and of course you want to score in the Premier League. I'm grateful to God for giving me the opportunity to score in the Championship and now I am grateful to him I can score in the Premier League. But, you know, I'm not going to get carried away with it, I just want to glorify God, I want to keep pushing and working hard every day to help my team win and score goals.

Do you set yourself targets as a striker?
I never really try to set a target as it then puts a lot of pressure on me. I just keep working and the most important thing is to be a team player; when the team wins a game, I am happy. If I score, then thanks to God, but if I don't, then I move on to the next game, working hard for the team.

How did you come to faith?

I was born in a Christian background in Nigeria. As a Christian, I believe in God and I have seen him do wonders in my life in many ways and on many occasions. Any time I get on my knees and pray to God, I see a difference. Everything I have, everything I have achieved today is because of the grace of God. I made a vow that all glory should be given back to God in my life. As someone who believes in God I know I am not perfect, but I do acknowledge that there is somebody out there who is keeping me going when I cry out to him.

On your Twitter page your bio says, 'My God is able.' What does this mean?

It means, my God is able to do all things. There is nothing that God cannot do. So I say, 'My God is able, able to do all things,' he created the heavens and the earth, he created the universe, he created the world we are in today, so there is nothing impossible for God. So that's what it's short for – my God is able.

What does your faith mean to you?

It means a lot to me. Not just on the pitch but in my life, everything I do. I have God first. I can't go out of the house in the morning without praying, thanking God for a new day. Some people cannot walk, some people cannot see or leave their homes, so every day I wake up and thank God for a new opportunity. I also do a special prayer before a game too, so my life is all about God and praying to him and thanking him. I'm trying to do my best, I read my Bible as well, I'm not perfect but I try and live my life for God.

What is it like to be a Christian in football?

Being a Christian in football for me is normal. I have a few other Christian teammates like Heurelho Gomes, he's a good Christian. Also, Ikechi Anya and Troy Deeney too. But you know, I believe in God, I don't care what anybody else says about it, I don't care if people criticize me; I believe in my God. Everything I have, is God. Everything I have done, is God. So I don't really mind what other people say.

Best moment of your career?

I'm having the best moment of my career now because every day I wake up and I see a new opportunity to live, it's an opportunity to accomplish something that I am yet to accomplish. I want to give God thanks for where I am today, because I wouldn't be here without him.

Who is the best player you have ever played with?

I've played with some great players! I've played with Antonio Di Natale, he's such a great player and a legend and I respect him a lot. I've played with Alexis Sánchez too. I've had the privilege to play with some great players and there are lots of fantastic ones in Watford too.

What does the future hold for Odion Ighalo?

Only God knows what the future holds. I just wake up each day and thank God for what he has done. I don't know what the future holds but I know that God is good and he knows my future.

'I am a Christian first and a footballer second'

Full name: **John Joseph Bostock**
DOB: 15 January 1992
Born: Camberwell, London
Clubs: Crystal Palace, Tottenham Hotspur, Brentford (loan), Hull City (loan), Sheffield Wednesday (loan), Swindon Town (loan), Toronto FC (loan), Royal Antwerp, OH Leuven
Position: Midfielder

Oud-Heverlee Leuven FC

John Bostock

What's it like being a professional footballer?
It's a real honour, it's the game I've loved from as young as I can remember, so to be a professional and to have the chance to do what I enjoy most is a real privilege.

When did you start playing football?
My earliest memories with a ball are when I joined my first team, Pelo FC, in south London, aged five, and then I signed for Palace after a trial a couple of years after.

What was it like making your debut at just 15 years old?
It's definitely one of the highlights of my career so far. My dad and I had been watching Palace for ten years as I had a season ticket from the age of five, so to make my debut for the club I supported and to break the record for the youngest player in the history of the club was amazing.

Regarded as one of the brightest young talents, what did you make of the hype surrounding your name?
It was nice to be regarded as a player with a bright future and to be recognized for the craft you put so much time and effort into. However, if you believe all the hype and only get encouraged when people say you are great, it only means you will be discouraged when they say you're not. So I've always tried to take the opinions of others with a pinch of salt.

What's the pressure like being a footballer?
Understandably, being judged by thousands of people on your performance every week brings some form of pressure, but you learn to deal with it and it helps massively knowing that I am a Christian first and footballer second, so regardless of my performance, I'm still accepted in Christ.

Why the move to Belgium?
When my contract expired at Spurs, I had several offers to move to clubs in England. However, at that time in my career I understood that

it wasn't about moving to the biggest club possible, it was about me rebuilding and moving somewhere where I would have the platform to show what I can do, to grow in confidence and really enjoy just playing every week again.

I had been on loan to different clubs and I realized it was important for me to find a footballing home to learn the game and improve. Jimmy Floyd Hasselbaink became the manager at Royal Antwerp FC, and he called me and said that he would love to have me in his team, so it was a no-brainer for me in making the decision to move to Belgium.

Was moving to Belgium hard?

Moving abroad comes with its challenges, but I've always believed that if you want something bad enough you will make sacrifices to achieve it. The hardest thing about playing abroad is being away from my family for really long periods, and missing my niece and nephews growing up because they grow up so quick. My wife has been a real blessing, and having her out in Belgium with me makes life a lot easier.

How did you become a Christian?

Growing up, I always knew there was something out there, but that was it really. My family weren't religious either. My main focus was football, so that kept me out of trouble and mischief while growing up in London.

However, my sister became a Christian when I was 16, and the way her life changed really made an impact on me. She invited me to church several times but I kindly declined, although one Sunday I decided to join her. That was the first time I heard the gospel. I realized that day that even though I was a good person in my own eyes, the bad news was that I had sinned more times in my life than I could count, and I needed to be forgiven and made right with God.

I repented of my sins and I accepted the fact that Jesus died for me and paid the price for my sins to be forgiven. That was over six years ago, and I thank God for saving me.

How do you deal with pressures in football as a Christian?
The best way to deal with the pressures that come in football is to spend quality time with the Lord. There is no substitute for prayer and reading the Scriptures every day. It's important to renew our minds and to realize that we don't have to do anything in our own strength but to lean on Jesus, who promises to strengthen us and carry our stress and worry.

Is it hard being a Christian in football?
It definitely comes with its challenges, but God equips and strengthens you to be able to do your best as a player and to represent him at the same time.

Do you have to conform to any stereotype as a footballer?
I think people automatically tend to taint footballers with the same brush. However, it's down to the individual to show that not everyone is the same. Personally I don't feel like I have to conform to any stereotype as a footballer. Even though I may look like other footballers, I'm different, and even though football is a huge part of my life, it's not the only thing that defines me.

What do your teammates say about your faith?
Some teammates have tried to have a laugh at me for being a Christian, but for the most part they are cool and respect me for my beliefs.

Favourite Bible verse?
My favourite verse in Philippians 3.8, 'Indeed, I count everything as loss because of the surpassing worth of knowing Christ Jesus my Lord. For his sake I have suffered the loss of all things and count them as rubbish, in order that I may gain Christ' (ESV). It's really powerful.

Favourite worship song?
My favourite worship song is 'In Christ Alone' and my Christian rap song is 'The Excellency of Christ' by Timothy Brindle.

2

Who are your footballing inspirations?

Ronaldinho is my favourite player, and growing up I spent hours watching him. I like the way Kaká carries himself on and off the pitch, and he is a great example of a Christian in sport.

What advice would you give to young aspiring players?

Don't be satisfied with being good, always look for ways to improve. Watch players you like on YouTube and try to copy the things they do on the pitch. Try to listen to the coaches and people around you and never underestimate practice, making the ball your best friend. You will have to make sacrifices to be what you want to be, but always be willing to give up what you are for what you can be.

Finally, what advice would you give to Christians who play football?

God gave you the talent to play football and put you in a club and around people to be an example and to represent Jesus to them. It's uncomfortable being different but don't be afraid or ashamed of the gospel and of what God has done in your life. Ask God to strengthen you to be a good example of someone whose life has been changed by the King of Kings.

'God gives you the talent and the rest is up to you'

Full name:	**Chuba Amechi Akpom**
DOB:	9 October 1995
Born:	Canning Town, London
Clubs:	Arsenal, Brentford (loan), Coventry City (loan), Nottingham Forest (loan), Hull City (loan)
Position:	Striker

Hull City FC

Chuba Akpom

Chuba, let's start at the beginning. What was it like to be snapped up by a huge club like Arsenal at such a young age?
It was good – obviously at first you just play football for the fun of it, and I didn't realize how big it was, but as you get older you start to realize that it's a massive club. Football gets more and more serious. It was a bit of a surprise – I had West Ham, Chelsea and Arsenal that came in for me at first and eventually I chose Arsenal because I grew up supporting them.

You have managed to break into the Arsenal first team on a few occasions. Is it a surreal feeling when you think you were only 17 at the time?
It was good – you know it's everyone's dream to play in the Premier League, and then to make my debut at such a young age was a crazy feeling. I came on for Olivier Giroud, which wasn't bad.

What's it like to be managed by a legend of the game – Arsène Wenger?
Yeah, it's crazy, he's such an experienced guy and a legend. To be managed by someone with so much experience is crazy – when I was at Arsenal I would see him every day at training.

Wenger has said in recent times that he believes you can make the step up to first-team football with the Gunners. Does this motivate you to make it happen?
Definitely – it gives you a breath of fresh air, like relief that he puts his confidence in you. He says it to me all of the time, he just says that I need to keep working hard when I go out on loan and then I will come back a better player. I have been in the first team for two years now and I have learnt so much from him so far.

Let's talk about England. You have come up through the youth ranks from U16s. Are you confident of kicking on to represent the senior side?
Yeah, definitely, I am confident, and I have just signed a new deal, so the next chance that I get, I've just got to take it.

What's your best XI of players you've played with?

Goalkeeper – Petr Čech
Left back – Luke Shaw
Centre back – Sead Hajroviæ
Centre back – Laurent Koscielny
Right back – Héctor Bellerin
Right midfielder – Alex Oxlade-Chamberlain
Centre midfielder – Tomás Rosický
Centre midfielder – Santi Cazorla
Left midfielder – Alexis Sánchez
Centre attacking midfielder – Jack Wilshere
Striker – Theo Walcott

**Chuba, you are very open about your Christian faith.
When did you first encounter God?**

I was brought up in a strong and religious house ever since I was
born. I always went to church from an early age and from about 16
it became my own faith. I go to church when I get time to, because
we have a lot of football going on. I make sure that I go around
Christmas and definitely around Easter.

**Do you feel that God has given you the global platform of
football so that you can make a big impact for him?**

Yes, I think that God gives you the talent and the rest is up
to you, because not everyone is talented enough to play football
but they all have their own gifts. God has given me the talent
and I have worked hard on top of that to get where I am now.

**Have you had any positive 'God chats' with teammates who
don't know God?**

Yeah, I had one with one of the England U21 boys a little while
ago. We were talking about the exact same thing, they were
asking 'Are you a footballer because of God or because of your
hard work?' I told them my thoughts about it and the whole team
was listening.

So who do you bounce off or chat to about your faith?
There's no one in particular, a few players at Arsenal do their prayers, for example Mesut Özil, he's religious. There are a few players but I just keep it to myself really and make sure to say my prayers before I go out on to the pitch. I pray a lot.

Does God feature in your pre-match routine?
Yeah definitely, before I step on the pitch, if you have watched me then you would probably notice, I pick up a blade of grass and then I do the sign of the cross. I do a short prayer before kick-off and if I score a goal I do the sign of the cross. When I have a bad game I pray and if I have a good game I pray. I guess if I have had a good game then I thank God for giving me the strength to score. If I don't have a good game then I pray that I would understand and that he'd help me in my next performance, to be better than the performance that I just gave.

'I always put God first'

Full name:	**Victor Mugubi Wanyama**
DOB:	25 June 1991
Born:	Nairobi, Kenya
Clubs:	Helsingborg, Beerschot, Celtic, Southampton
Position:	Midfielder

Matt Watson/Southampton FC

Victor Wanyama

When you first started playing football, did you ever dream of making it as a professional?
That was only a dream, but I used to pray that it would happen one day. Being raised in a Christian family, I was taught to go to church and pray about things happening in my life, so I'd always give them over to God.

What was it like signing for Scottish champions Celtic in 2011?
It meant so much. They are such a big team. For me also, I was the first Kenyan to be signed by them. I didn't mind the fact that not many people had heard of me. Celtic was just the perfect choice, they are a religious club, they look after and help a lot of people. It was a high standard of playing so it was a good thing for me.

What was it like playing in the Champions League?
It was great to play in the Champions League. Celtic Park was just unbelievable, the fans are something else. I would say that playing in the Champions League for Celtic at Celtic Park is the best place to play football.

Highlight at Celtic?
It has to be when we beat Barcelona in the Champions League and on top of that, I managed to score as well. That was a great night.

From Celtic, you joined Southampton. Why the move?
It was a brilliant move, I just wanted to test myself again but this time in the Premier League. It's another fantastic club, another Christian club and the chance to play in the best league in the world was an opportunity I couldn't say no to.

With a big transfer fee attached to your name, do you feel the pressure?
I think for me, there's no pressure. The media and fans always put pressure on players when they move, especially when there's a lot of

money involved. However, it was only a matter of time before I settled and I'm just getting my head down now and working hard for my club.

Best moment so far at Southampton?
I have had a few. Scoring the winning goals against Hull City and Swansea, they were pretty special. Also, finishing seventh in the 2014/2015 Premier League season, plus we reached 60 points, which I think was a new record for us, so that was amazing too.

Best XI you've ever played with (including yourself of course)?
Wow, this is a tough one. I've played with some fantastic players, but I think this team would have to be some of the best players I've been able to play with.

    Goalkeeper – Fraser Forster
    Right back – Nathaniel Clyne
    Left back – Charlie Mulgrew
    Centre back – José Fonte
    Centre back – Kelvin Wilson
    Left midfielder – Joe Ledley
    Centre midfielder – Victor Wanyama
    Centre midfielder – Ki Sung-yeung
    Right midfielder – Saido Mané
    Striker – Gary Hooper
    Striker – Rickie Lambert

Best player you've ever played with?
I will say, Rickie Lambert – he was such an unbelievable player to work with, just fantastic.

If you could play with any centre midfielder, past or present, who would it be and why?
Andrés Iniesta, because he can make those key passes and he is just fantastic on the ball. He can push forward and join the attacks

while I can sit and hold the midfield a bit more. He would get so many assists; I think it would be a good partnership!

Victor, tell us how you became a Christian?
As I said before, I was born into a Christian family and my mum used to take me along to church from a young age, and that's when I first experienced and met God. Even now, I believe that before I start my day, I need to give it over to God in prayer. If I don't put God first, things become hard. I believe that through him, things can go well, and that's why I always put God first.

Do you have any other Christian players you connect with?
Before, at Celtic, I used to speak a lot with the likes of Emilio Izaguirre and Efe Ambrose. They were two good Christian guys who I used to speak to a lot. But here at Southampton, I don't think there are any other Christian guys in the team. Sometimes I have players come up to me and ask questions, which is great, while others just respect my beliefs.

Finally, do you have a favourite piece of Scripture that encourages you?
I have a lot of favourite verses, but one I like to put in me every day is John 3.16, 'For God so loved the world that he gave his one and only Son, that whoever believes in him shall not perish but have eternal life.' Any time I just want to think about something, like why are we here, why do we live or what is our purpose, I fill my heart with this verse and it inspires me.

'I had put all my hope in football'

Full name: **Gavin Keith Peacock**
DOB: 18 November 1967
Born: Eltham, London
Clubs: Gillingham, Bournemouth, Queens Park Rangers,
            Newcastle United, Chelsea, Charlton Athletic.
            Retired in 2002
Position: Midfielder

Jard Harfield/Calvary Grace

Gavin Peacock

So Gavin, most people will either know you for your football playing days at Chelsea or your TV punditry, but let's go back to the beginning. Growing up, was it always going to be football?

It was, I was brought up in a footballing family. My dad, Keith, played for Charlton Athletic for 17 years in the 1960s and 70s, and so I grew up at the Valley watching him play. All I ever thought about doing was following in my dad's footsteps. That was the goal for me, like a lot of schoolboys, that was the dream. Of course I had someone like my dad who could be a hands-on coach from an early age.

Looking back, what would you say was your career highlight as a player?

Well I didn't win things like so many great players have won, for me though there were a few things. Getting promotion with Newcastle was great, getting to the FA Cup Final with Chelsea in 1994 was great, but I think the highlight of that season was the two goals that I scored against Manchester United, home and away. A personal one would have been for one game only, scoring two goals against Luton in the semi-final of the FA Cup in 1994. We won 2–0 and we played it at Wembley.

Who is the best player you've played with and why?

I played with some great players, like Ruud Gullit, Mark Hughes, Gianluca Vialli and Gianfranco Zola, but I still maintain that Glenn Hoddle was the best one I played with. He was a maestro. Kevin Keegan called me up when I left Newcastle and he said that I would learn more from playing with Glenn in training than anyone else, and that certainly was the case. It was as if Glenn had this computerized mind that could see everything on the field, pick the most dangerous option and make the perfect pass. I learnt a lot from Glenn. I would say he had the best football mind.

Now let's reverse that: best player you ever played against?

The best player I ever played against in my time? I'd plump for Eric Cantona, just from my time in the Premier League. For a period there

I thought he just had something special, Manchester United were a great team and it was a great era for them. He was the linchpin, the key; he not only had great ability, he had great strength and power and he just had this awesome presence on the field.

You said in interview 'Football was my God as a youngster but it didn't satisfy, I was empty.' What did you mean by this?

I always wanted to be a footballer, like a lot of schoolboys did. I then got that and achieved that goal. Suddenly I am a professional footballer at 18 years old, I am playing for QPR in the top division, I've got money in my pocket, I've got a nice car, I've got a career, I've got a little bit of fame growing as it were, and yet I wasn't satisfied. I wasn't happy – if I played well I was up but if I played badly I was down, because I had put all my hope in football.

Then I just went along to the local church that I was living near with my parents at the time, and I went one Sunday evening. I heard the minister preach but he invited me back to his house after for a youth meeting and I thought that I'd pop along there, I didn't expect too much. When I walked into that youth meeting there were maybe six young people my own age there and I walked in with everything the world says will bring you happiness and success. I walked in and then heard them talk about Jesus Christ and then I heard them pray and there was a reality to their faith and a joy that I didn't have. I thought, like a lot of people, 'Yeah, God's up there somewhere,' and that I would shoot up a prayer if I was in a bit of trouble – it had no bearing on my life. So it was then that I began to hear the gospel and the gospel means good news, so I repented and trusted in Jesus Christ.

Do you have a Bible verse you particularly cherish or always go back to?

I think Matthew 6, when Jesus says to not worry about tomorrow, tomorrow will have enough worries of its own, and it's a passage where he is talking about how God clothed the flowers in the field, he feeds the birds in the air, how much more his children? It says how much more is he going to care for you now that you are a child of God, and for me being in such a precarious job where you could lose your career with one tackle in football, to know that God is for me and that he is going to take care of me was great security to me.

In what is such a materialistic and money-driven industry, how hard was it to be a professional footballer and a Christian?
Well, as you say, it's a money-driven career. I earned good money, I didn't earn the money that they do now at Chelsea, so Dennis Wise and I used to go and battle for an extra £50 on our win bonus. Jesus says that the love of money is the root of all kinds of evil, not necessarily having money, so it's then what you do with it and how you use it. Do you love it or can you hold these things up to God? For me, being a Christian and a footballer, I am in a local church and hearing the word of God, reading the Bible myself and am around other Christians. It's very important because you are being encouraged and then other Christians keep you grounded even when there may have been certain temptations to move off course.

At what point did you know God was calling you into church ministry?
When I retired from football in 2002, I actually went into the media for a while with the BBC, and that was going quite well, very well in fact. I was really enjoying it but the Lord powerfully called me to ministry around 2005–06, and I really sensed a call to teach this word, so I was given some opportunities to preach and did some studies at Cambridge University, in Old Testament and New Testament studies. It was then I knew that I needed to give it up [the BBC] because I wanted time to prepare properly for pastoral ministry. Then I decided that I could do it in England or I could look at leaving the country away from the public profile. We had been going to Canada for a little while, so after some prayer and some thinking, my wife and I decided to move there in 2008.

How often do you slip your football playing days into your sermons?

I have maybe mentioned it a couple of times, in terms of if it fits the passage. I will use certain metaphors but good preaching demands that the passage dictates and then the illustrations should come, short and sharp, out of that. So if it fits, now and again, but if not, then I won't.

5

'God features in my everyday life'

Full name:	**Benik Tunani Afobe**
DOB:	12 February 1993
Born:	Leyton, London
Clubs:	Arsenal, Huddersfield Town (loan), Reading (loan), Bolton Wanderers (loan), Millwall (loan), Sheffield Wednesday (loan), MK Dons (loan), Wolves, Bournemouth
Position:	Striker

Sam Bagnall/Wolves FC

Benik Afobe

You were signed by Arsenal at the age of six. When did it sink in for you that you could make it as a professional?

When I first started playing football it was just about enjoying it, sport and fitness, and loving the game. Then the time came, at maybe 10 or 11, when I thought 'Do you know what? I may have a chance here.' The first few years were about enjoying it, and then you start going to Arsenal games and realize you play for the same club as Thierry Henry – just the younger version! You watch those players and think you want to be like them, and that is when it all really started for me and really sunk in.

Arsenal sent you out on loan to a host of different clubs. How hard was it to keep moving from club to club as a footballer?

It was difficult because I never really had stability. I became good friends with teammates and then before you know it there are only two weeks left of the loan! It was always a case of having to quickly adapt to new players and how they play. I much prefer being settled at a club and knowing the philosophy of the club and getting to love the club. The loans did help me a lot in giving me experience and living away from home and being at teams that were successful, others not so successful, and with all the different styles of play. It helped me grow a lot in the early stages of my career.

Career highlight so far?

Scoring twice for MK Dons against Manchester United in the Capital One Cup. That was the game I burst on to the scene. There was a lot of talk when I was at Arsenal about my potential as a young English striker who had the capability of scoring goals. Then I went out on loan and had injuries and other loans when I didn't play, so I was wondering when I might get a chance to shine. Then I got those goals against Manchester United and became the talk of the town. That just gave me so much confidence and I just carried on from there.

Was it hard to leave Arsenal?

It was hard in the sense that Arsenal was all I had known. I had been there from the age of six and they became like my second family. The staff, the players, the club – I never fell out with anyone at Arsenal and have a lot of friends there to this day. So it was hard in that sense. However, I also knew that if I wanted to be a top player at the highest level, for my career the right thing to do was to leave. I felt at home at Wolves – everyone there treated me well and hopefully I have repaid them with my performances and my goals.

Who was the best player at Arsenal when you were there?
Wow – how can I pick? I'd go for Cesc Fàbregas, Robin Van Persie and Samir Nasri. I was lucky enough to train with so many great players. I just missed out on Mesut Özil and Alexis Sánchez because I wasn't there when they came in. Jack Wilshere is up there as well. He is a good friend of mine and is a top player.

Best player you've ever played with?
In an actual game, I'd say Robin Van Persie. I played alongside him in a pre-season friendly. As a forward-thinking player I would go for him, as that was a great experience.

Do you believe you can be one of the best strikers in England and why?
Yes I think you have to believe that. If I didn't have aspirations to play at the highest level one day then I wouldn't really have carried on playing. You look at some of the best strikers in England at the moment – Jamie Vardy, Odion Ighalo, Harry Kane – they have all come through having played in the lower leagues at some stage. It has taken them time to get there but they have worked hard and are now proving themselves in the Premier League. They deserve all the respect for that and it is an example for people like me that if I keep working hard and believing in myself then I also have a chance. I definitely believe that I can be up there but it is about going out there and doing it, and I know I still have a long way to go. I won't be getting ahead of myself.

Benik Afobe

If you could have any strike partner in the world, past or present, who would it be and why?
It has to be the Brazilian Ronaldo. I was watching him on YouTube again the other day. He's unbelievable. He had everything and was the ideal centre forward. He did suffer with injuries and his lifestyle was maybe not quite as good as it could have been for someone at the top of his profession, however, his talent was unbelievable.

Can you share your testimony with us?
I was lucky enough to be born into a Christian family, but there comes a point when your mum and your dad can't just keep telling you about God. You have to really take it on yourself. That happened to be maybe when I was about 14 or 15 and started to read the Bible more, however, there is no point reading it without understanding. So I also started to pray and ask God to give me the wisdom and the knowledge to understand and to be smart. God knows no one is perfect but I am trying to be the best person that I can be. I am trying every day to do that, to get better, and to one day spread the word of God not just to people who are suffering but others who need to get to God.

Do you share your faith with any of your teammates? If so, what do they say about your faith?
I actually prayed with Matt Doherty, one of my old teammates. He is also from a Christian family and we will sometimes pray and watch sermons on YouTube. Everyone thinks that we might meet up and just play FIFA but we also watch sermons. I know Sheyi Ojo is also a Christian and Kortney Hause. I wouldn't necessarily go around talking to the other lads about God but I am happy to do so, and everyone knows what I think about God in my life.

Why is your faith so important to you?
It is very important to me, and that is all the time. I think God has helped me a lot in my football as well as in life and in trying to be the best person I can be. It's about having that faith and knowing God will look after you even when things are tough. When you think you

are down and out there is always light at the end of the tunnel.
There have been times in my football career when people may have
doubted me or I've had injuries. But I always knew that light in the
tunnel would always come, even though I still have a lot more
improvements to make.

How does God feature in your preparation for a match?
God features in my everyday life and that doesn't change on the day
of a match. I don't pray before a match, for example. I pray every
morning and every night and speak to God during the day. It is not
just about the match. Sometimes when I score I might do the sign
of the cross but it's not about God just being there on a matchday.
I live my life the same way whether I am playing football or not, and
so nothing is different on a matchday.

Favourite Bible verse?
Matthew 7.7 is one I like and was reading the other day: 'seek
and you will find; knock and the door will be opened to you.' Also,
Proverbs 3.6, about acknowledging God and him then guiding you.
It's just about having faith and knowing that God will never forsake
you – that is the theme of my favourite verses. And Romans 8.31 –
'If God is for us, who can be against us?' That is another one I think
about a lot.

'I'm inspired by God who gives me strength'

Full name: **Christian Atsu Twasam**
DOB: 10 January 1992
Born: Ada Foah, Ghana
Clubs: Porto, Rio Ave (loan), Vitesse Arnhem (loan), Everton (loan),
            Bournemouth (loan), Málaga (loan), Chelsea
Position: Midfielder

Christian Atsu

Christian, as a young boy, who was your footballing hero when you were growing up in Ghana?

When I was growing up in Ghana the one I was looking up to was Lionel Messi. I think he is the greatest footballer and I think that he is also very humble and has a great attitude.

So at the age of 17 you joined Portuguese giants Porto. That must have been a life-changing move for you.

It was a very difficult decision for me to make. My parents wouldn't allow me at first but I had to speak the truth that it was a big opportunity for my career. When I went there everything was different – the weather, the language, everything. It was a very hard life in Portugal but as time went on I was becoming better and getting used to the people and the weather. Right now I am very happy because FC Porto took very good care of me and I really appreciate what they did for me.

Was manager André Villas-Boas key to your development as a young player?

I was in the junior side while he was coaching there, so he brought me into the first team and I trained with them. He gave me the opportunity to train with players like Hulk, Radamel Falcao and also James Rodríguez. So it was great for my confidence level – every time I trained with them and then went back to the junior side, I felt more and more confident.

So moving forward, was it an easy decision to go to Chelsea?

I think it was a really difficult decision for me to move to Chelsea because it was a new side. It was very difficult but I moved there because it was my dream to play in the English Premier League. When the opportunity came to move there, I had to take it – no matter what anyone said, I had to do everything to achieve my dream.

Let's name your ultimate XI of players you have played with, yourself included.

    Goalkeeper – Tim Howard
    Left back – Baba Rahman
    Right back – Harrison Afful
    Centre back – Jonathan Mensah
    Centre back – Bruno Alves
    Centre midfielder – Wakaso
    Centre midfielder – João Moutinho
    Centre attacking midfielder – James Rodríguez
    Left attacking midfielder – Christian Atsu
    Right attacking midfielder – Hulk
    Striker – Asamoah Gyan

Who would you say is the best player you've ever played against?

In the World Cup with Ghana I played against Cristiano Ronaldo – he was just unbelievable.

You were named the best player at the 2015 African Cup of Nations. How proud are you of this accolade?

First, I thank God for giving me the opportunity to play in the African Cup. I am really proud of how far I have come and it was a great moment for me, most of all for my family and also for my career. It gives me motivation in my football career so I am really proud and happy for that moment.

Shifting the focus now, tell us about how you came to know Jesus?

I knew Jesus through my parents when I was growing up. They would be talking in the way of Christ and preaching the gospel to me. I think they did a great job because Jesus is the best thing that ever happened in my life, and I give thanks to my parents for how they brought me up to know him. My parents wanted me to be a very good Christian because they knew the importance of it.

41

In your Twitter bio you put 'God is my inspiration, sport is my passion and success is my motivation.' Tell us what this means for you.

I think for me I'm inspired by God, who gives me strength each and every day to move forward in my football career. Sport is my passion. I love sports and I have passion for playing football. The last one is that success is my motivation. I want to be successful because I think that if you are a Christian, you're a man of God and you have to be successful. It will be difficult but you will, because God is your strength. God is not a failure and I am motivated to be successful.

Are there any other Christian footballers you touch base with?

When I went to Bournemouth there were a few Christians in their team – Junior Stanislas, who plays for them, is a good friend of mine and we went to church together. You can see on my Instagram page that I took a picture with the pastor, so I sometimes hang out with him too. We would go to church together and we share the word of God. Also in the Ghana national team I am always in a room with Jonathan Mensah, and he is also a good Christian. When we go away with the national team, in the night we have to praise God and when we wake up we have to thank God, so with him it is great because we motivate each other.

Do you believe your footballing talent is a gift from God?

Yes, for me it's not just football, it's not just football talent. I believe all the talents that people have come from God because he gives them to us and he wants us to be successful in our talents. It's not something that just happens, it is God who gives these talents to everyone.

What advice would you give to other Christian footballers making their way in the game?

The only advice that I can give to them is that we all want to be successful in football, but we should not forget that it is not only football that we are playing. We have God in the life we live, outside of football – we don't just pray for God to just help us play football.

We ask God to help us to be good people, to be kind and to live a Christian life. It is about how you treat people, so we should not forget that we are not just playing football but we are also living a Christian life. The reason I am saying this is because people pray to God to give them something. But what if my football doesn't work? Does that mean that God didn't listen to my prayers? No. It doesn't mean that. What is important is that we know God is always there to worship, even if we fail in our career. We will not be shaken in our belief in God.

'Do everything for the glory of God'

Full name:	**Paul-José M'poku Ebunge**
DOB:	19 April 1992
Born:	Kinshasa, Zaïre (now Democratic Republic of Congo)
Clubs:	Tottenham Hotspur, Leyton Orient (loan), Standard Liège, Cagliari (loan), Chievo
Position:	Midfielder

Paul-José M'poku

So to kick off, growing up, at what point did you think: 'I want to be a pro footballer'?
I think when I was young, around the age of five, I started playing on the streets and my dad was taking me to play. From the beginning I watched football on TV, and when I was going to play on the streets everyone would say that I was still young, but when you are at the age of ten, twelve, then you are starting to play better. From there I thought: 'That's what I want to do, that's what I want to be.'

So at that point, who was your dream club to play for one day?
My dream team had always been Real Madrid because I liked the players, and at the time they had Beckham, Ronaldo and Figo. I loved to watch the team, especially because Zidane was there on top of that.

What was it like moving to a huge club like Tottenham at a young age?
It was a big dream for me because I was just 15 years old and a club like Tottenham came to me and wanted me. At that age I didn't know what to do but I made the decision to go, and it was one of the best decisions I made in my life.

You've spent the biggest part of your career to date at Standard Liège in Belgium. What's been your personal highlight?
Playing for your home town is one of the biggest things that everybody dreams of, to play where you grew up – it's so special. And for me, Standard Liège will always be special.

Being quite a well-travelled footballer already, what is the best league you have played in?
Well I am only 23 and I have already played maybe 100 games in the first division. Obviously I was at Tottenham, where I had one game on the bench in the Cup but didn't play in the Premier League. It's different, Italy is different, I think Serie A is better than Belgium because there are bigger clubs and players so perhaps for that reason I would say Serie A. Belgium is a good league for getting strength and fitness.

If you weren't a footballer, what would you be doing?

I don't know actually, seriously, I don't know – it has always been football.

We know there's more to you than just your football career. Tell us how you became a Christian?

I gave my life to Jesus when I went to a concert event where there was a pastor who shared his testimony. I found it touching because at that time I came to England and didn't speak English. I had my best friend John Bostock with me, and this one time I saw him praying, now for me I grew up as a Christian but it was never personal to me. I grew up going to church, my mum was Catholic and so I grew up knowing God, that he was real. However, I wasn't really in it, I didn't give my life to God but just knew that there was a God. So then I saw John Bostock praying and I asked, 'Are you a Christian?' And he said, 'Yeah,' and so he invited me to his church and that's how I became a Christian really. God really brought us together.

Is it difficult being a Christian combined with the glamorous lifestyle that comes with being a pro footballer?

I think the Holy Spirit makes it easier but it's still not easy, because in the football world there are girls, money and this and that. You are around all these things so you hear what is happening and you hear what others do. By God's grace I continue to be there, to pray and try to make a difference.

Do you have a favourite Bible verse that encourages you?

Yeah, it's 1 Corinthians 10.31, 'whether you eat or drink or whatever you do, do it all for the glory of God.' That's my favourite verse because I think it's just perfect – do everything for the glory of God, don't do it for man or anyone else, do it for him.

Paul-José, you and some other Christian footballers have set up a group called 'Ballers in God'. Tell us why that came about.

John Bostock had been praying about it and then he shared this with me and I agreed that it could be good. It is really just to encourage one another. Plus there are many Christians in France and Belgium and we just want to encourage each other and pray for each other. If John is going through a tough time, like the Bible says: iron sharpens iron, and that's what we really want to do.

Finally, what does the future hold for you?
I don't know, I just want to play football and then see where God's going to take me. I did have some opportunity to come back to the Premier League. However, if I was to go back I want to go back to a good club with a good contract and not just come back to be in the Premier League. It is important for me to play most weeks but I can't really do anything but work hard and see what God wants me to do. I think the next step after Chievo would be to play in the Champions League or Europa League. I will see.

'My performance is unto God because that's who I want to glorify'

Full name:	**Darren Mark Moore**
DOB:	22 April 1974
Born:	Birmingham, England
Clubs:	Torquay United, Doncaster Rovers, Bradford City, Portsmouth, West Bromwich Albion, Derby County, Barnsley, Burton Albion. Retired in 2012
Position:	Defender

Darren Moore

You've played for a host of clubs in your career. How would you sum up your time in football?
I'm very pleased and thankful for the long career I had. I've got no complaints whatsoever, I have 20 years of fantastic memories and to go with those memories, some successful periods. Obviously there have been some highs and some lows but all in all I cannot complain at all. I'm very thankful and feel a blessed man with my playing career, and now that has gone on to the coaching side. If I can have as much longevity and success on the coaching side as I did as a player, then I'll be a very happy and fulfilled man.

Tell us what it was like to play in the Premier League with some of the world's best players?
Fantastic. One of my ambitions when I started on the long road of football was to play at the highest level possible that the game had to offer. When I started, that was the old First Division, and that then quickly developed into the Premier League. So to achieve that was a dream come true, and to play at that level meant so much, coming up against some of the best players in the world. It's something that I value right up until this day.

Best moment of your career?
My career highlight was scoring one of the first goals of the day against Crystal Palace, which took us to the Premier League with West Bromwich Albion. Obviously, I had achieved promotion a few years before that with Bradford, but I hadn't physically made my debut for them, so for me it has to be the goal and promotion for West Brom. Another nice moment for me was when I was in the Premier League with West Brom and I scored the goal against Fulham that earned us three valuable points that season.

In contrast, then, what's been one of the toughest moments of your career and how did you deal with that?
One of the hardest moments of my career was suffering a cruciate knee ligament injury, playing against Chelsea. I went to play a ball in the channel against Jimmy Floyd Hasselbaink and I just pulled up

short to read the bounce of the ball and my studs got caught in the turf and snapped my cruciate. So that was a real low – being out of the game for nine to ten months is a big miss for any player who suffers an injury. On the other hand, I accepted the Lord into my life in 1999, and along the way through my injury I remember thinking, 'I'm not going to accept what doctors have been saying that my career is over.' I put my trust in the Lord whom I trust and serve. I remember after the game in which I got the injury, I got dropped off at my pastor's house so he could lay hands on me and pray for me. I gained strength from that and I grew in confidence just days after suffering the knee injury. The recovery ended up being straightforward, but I had to put my strength on the Lord during that time. Saying that, it's not just the bad times that I rely on God – I also give him thanks and praise during the good times as well.

Who would you say is the best player you've had the privilege of playing with?
Wow, that's a difficult one. I mean, Nwankwo Kanu was class. We all saw him when he was at Arsenal, but when he came to West Brom, he was just an incredibly talented footballer and a wonderful man. He is right up there with ability and he can do anything with the ball. He's a world-class player. I remember playing in a game, I think it was Dennis Bergkamp's 400th appearance for Arsenal, and Kanu played on that day – and I tell you now, if he hadn't played, we would not have won that game. He turned up and single-handedly destroyed Arsenal; we ended up beating them 2–1 at the Hawthorns and he was incredible.

Who's the best striker you ever came up against in your time as a central defender?
There's too many to name! I've played against the likes of Fernando Torres, Michael Owen, Alan Shearer, Carlos Tevez, Mark Viduka, Wayne Rooney and Cristiano Ronaldo. But if I had to pick one player, it would have to be Thierry Henry. He would be the one who was the exceptional player. I'm talking about an era where there were strikers coming out of every corner, but in all that he was the standout

performer. The way he moved, carried the ball, his pace and eye for a goal; he was just exceptional.

How proud are you of representing Jamaica at international level?

It was a wonderful experience. Especially for my mother and father. It was such a treasured experience for me. I managed to play overseas in some brilliant games, and even though I only have three caps, I played in many friendlies with the Jamaican team. I had a wonderful time there and it really helped me develop and mould into a better player when I returned to my club.

Since retiring you've remained in football. Tell us about your new role at West Brom.

My professional job title is Professional Development Phase Coach. What I do is work across the different age groups at the club. Since Tony Pulis came in as manager, I've been drafted into working with the first team, which is great. My ambition is to go as high as I possibly can in the world of coaching. At the moment I'm at a Premier League club coaching and developing some of the elite players, which is great. I'm there to help develop that transition between U21 level and the first team, and it's going really well at the moment. I also help out with the loan players who have left the club to seek first-team football. I help guide those players to find a way into our first team when they return.

How did you become a Christian?

It was back in 1999 when I was at Bradford City. I remember we were coming back from Doncaster that day and I was travelling with a teammate who is a dear friend of mine to this very day, Wayne Jacobs. We used to share in the car together. I remember one day he was sharing to me about God and I said to him, 'I don't think you can serve God and be a professional footballer at the same time.' How wrong I was! For Wayne, that was his cue-card, if you like, to sharing his faith with me, and we'd read from the UCB's The Word for Today together, which gave key Bible verses to think about. On this one particular day the verse said, 'The Lord said he does not give us a spirit of fear, but of love and a sound mind.' At that time, when I got this verse, I was at Bradford and having a difficult time. I wasn't very confident and I was worried about my ability, that I wouldn't be able to make the step up from League Two to League One. But when I shared that with Wayne he said, 'I really believe this verse is for you Darren, and God knows your heart.'

From that moment, it just went on from there. We had Christians in Sport meetings, where we'd share from the Bible together. Before this encounter I was scared to play, but from that moment on I used to look forward to matches and I was playing some of my best football. There was one game against Bolton Wanderers, when we were bottom of the league and they were top. We ended up drawing the game 2–2 and I was voted man of the match. From that point on, for the next 30 games, we ended up, from in the relegation places, to getting promotion that season, and I was then voted in the PFA Divisional XI – it's one of the biggest professional accolades in the game. I put all that down to God and being able to share with other Christian guys, and that's when I committed my life to Christ.

Would you say you see yourself as a role model for other Christians?
During my playing days, no. I was just getting on with my career. However, I would say that I see myself as more of a role model now for other Christians. God gets all my praise for where I've been and where I am at now.

Do you think prayer helps performance?
I think it can help from a mental perspective. Personally, I never used to pray for my performance. I would always pray for safety and provision over the fans and the players; I'd pray a prayer of blessing and protection over the stadium. I never ever prayed for a result. My performance is unto God because that's who I want to glorify. Also, in terms of a professional, it states in our contracts that we must adhere to playing to the best of our ability for the football club at all times. So

I always had a policy that my ability might sometimes be wanting; my passing or heading might be a bit off, but I'd never let anyone ever question my work rate and commitment to the club.

Favourite Bible verse?
I think 2 Timothy 1.7, 'For God has not given us a spirit of fear, but of power and of love and of a sound mind' (NKJV). That verse just opened my eyes to Christianity and helped me ask questions that resulted in me finding the Lord.

'My essence will not change and my essence is Jesus'

Full name: **Ricardo Izecson dos Santos Leite**
DOB: 22 April 1982
Born: São Paulo, Brazil
Clubs: São Paulo, A.C. Milan, Real Madrid, Orlando City
Position: Midfielder

Ricardo Kaká

Everyone knows about the passion of Brazilian football. What was it like playing in the midst of that at São Paulo?

It was amazing, I'm so thankful to God because he gave me far more than I could ever want or imagine. Everything that happened with São Paulo, A.C. Milan, Real Madrid, Orlando City and the Brazilian national team, it's all been such a great experience for me. My faith is growing in every city and every situation that I go through and São Paulo was amazing. My career is just a way of God allowing me to learn his ways.

In 2003, A.C. Milan came calling – how did it feel to be wanted by such a huge European club?

It was amazing, I always wanted to play in a special team in Europe. When I was a kid I always had a dream and thought to myself, 'I'd love to play for that team'; I just wanted to play in a big European team. When Milan made an offer to São Paulo, I went to the president and told him, 'Look, it's a great opportunity for me, it's not about money, I don't care if you can pay more than Milan, I just want to go there and play for this big team.' It was also such a big thing for São Paulo too, because they could then say that they have had one of their players playing for a huge team in Europe. They eventually agreed with me and sold me to Milan where my career in Italy started.

How do you balance your identity of being both a global football star worshipped by many and a child of God who worships Jesus?

I always try to be a transparent guy. The guy who is speaking to you right now will be the same guy if you came to meet me. The same goes for my career: if I play for a big team or if I win Player of the Year, for me it's just an opportunity to be grateful because I know it isn't me, it's God who lives in me and gives me the talent to play. God gave me everything and I want to give him the thanks and glory back to him. Of course, I have to work and improve my talent, be disciplined and persevering, but I have to have faith as well. The most important thing is knowing the one who gave me this talent, God.

Talk us through the Champions League final with Liverpool. Why did you reveal that shirt, 'I belong to Jesus', which has now become so iconic?

I always put a target in every part of my life, including my football career. One of my goals in terms of my career is to say to the world, 'I belong to Jesus.' It started in my house with my family, then I told my country and now I can say that I am showing the whole world. In fact, one of the first times that I used that jersey was back in the 2002 World Cup with Brazil and it's for those moments when people are looking for me. In that moment, I don't want people to see me, I want them to see Jesus. In that game against Liverpool when we were made champions and everyone was watching us, I wanted to use that moment to tell the world that I belong to Jesus.

What are some spiritual disciplines in your life that help you with your relationship with Jesus?

Well, the most important thing for me is to have conviction. I know what is the most important thing for me and that is Jesus. Jesus is my focus every time; in every situation I go through in life, the foundation of those decisions is made from my relationship with him. I'll be honest, I have had a lot of opportunities with women or money, but my faith and family have helped me so much by showing me what really matters. For me, what really matters is eternal life in heaven. I can have nice things but it's just a little pleasure, I feel really convicted that I don't want these pleasures, instead I want eternal life with Jesus.

How much did it mean to you, winning the Ballon d'Or and FIFA World Player of the Year in 2007?

It meant a lot! I never thought I could ever be the best player in the world. When I was young as a kid, I watched these players playing for these huge clubs and their national teams, and all of a sudden I was there with them. I was the best player in the world, it was just amazing. I was just there because of my teammates. I was merely a part of the puzzle. We had just won the Champions League with Milan and it was down to my teammates that I won that award, so I am so thankful that God put people in my life that helped me achieve that.

You went on to play for Real Madrid before making your way to America. Why did you move to MLS?
I had the chance to come and play for Orlando City and I just wanted to be a part of this moment in the league. I probably won't be playing during the best part of the MLS as it continues to grow, but I wanted to be a part of this moment right now. I think moving to the USA has been important for me in my spiritual life as well and I'm just so happy that I came here to play.

Who is the best player you've ever played with?
Oh yes, the best player I have ever played with has to be Ronaldo. I played with him at Real Madrid, A.C. Milan and for the national team. He is an amazing player and an amazing man too, he really helped me a lot and I just love the guy. The things I saw Ronaldo do on the pitch were incredible and that's why he's the best player I have ever played with.

How did you become a Christian?
I grew up in a Christian family, my mother and father are both Christians and they taught me all the values of the Bible and the love of Jesus. I grew up in that kind of environment. I then started to have my own experiences with God which are continuing now, but one day I just had to decide whether I believed it myself. I did, so I gave my life to Jesus.

What difference does faith make in your football career?
It makes a huge difference in my career. When I had bad moments with Madrid and the national team, my faith gave me the strength and support to keep fighting and helped me through those storms. I believed that something good was coming and it helped me learn from every situation. My faith is so important in every aspect of my career.

Do you connect with other Christian players?
Yes, here at Orlando City we have a few Christian guys. Andy Searles, our club chaplain, is such a nice guy, he runs our chapel

before games where we all pray together. If we play against other teams with Christian players, we can speak a little bit about what God is doing in our lives. With our national team, I often speak with David Luiz and Lucas as well as lots of other guys. It's not just in football though, I connect with Christians in other sports too and it's good to hear about what God is doing with them.

Do you have a favourite Bible verse?
No, I love the gospels and I love to speak about Jesus. Different verses and books mean more to me during different periods of my life. Sometimes verses speak more to me at different stages of my life than others.

If you could make one statement to those who see you as a role model, what would it be?
I would just say that Jesus is the best thing that could ever happen in our lives.

Football is a short career that doesn't last for ever. Have you any indications as to how God wants to use you after your career?
As I said before, football is just a way of God using me for his glory. He's using my career in football to test me and improve my faith for another big purpose and that purpose is eternity. Of course, football is important and I enjoy it and everything that comes with it, but I know that in two, three, four years, my career will be over but my life carries on. I will carry on into a new career but my essence will not change and my essence is Jesus.

'I realize that God gave me this gift'

Full name: **Samuel Oluwaseyi Ameobi**
DOB: 1 May 1992
Born: Newcastle upon Tyne, England
Clubs: Newcastle United, Middlesbrough (loan), Cardiff City (loan)
Position: Midfielder

Cardiff City FC

Sammy Ameobi

Sammy, who was your footballing idol growing up?
My footballing idol growing up was and still is Zinedine Zidane, the way he moved the ball with such grace was magical to me and his mind was always thinking a few steps ahead before even receiving it. For me he is the greatest player of all time.

Describe the feeling when you signed for Newcastle United. How did that move come about?
As a kid, football never really interested me and I didn't know much about the game, until the night when I first saw my brother, Shola, at 18 years old making his Premier League debut for Newcastle against Chelsea, back in 2000. I was eight at the time and I still remember going into school the next day thinking, 'All I want to do now is become a professional footballer' – all other dreams were out the window. So when I was ten I joined Walker Central boys club, the same club Shola played for growing up, then at the age of 14 I was brought into Newcastle United's academy by the same scout who spotted Shola and brought him to the club.

Four years down the line, not long after my eighteenth birthday, I made my Premier League debut against Chelsea, funnily enough, and Shola was actually playing in that game too, which was a proud day for my whole family. A dream I've had for ten years finally coming to pass – there's really no way to describe the feeling, but I know I will never forget it.

What's it like having an older brother who also plays professional football? Did you feel the pressure of expectation or was Shola helpful?
Growing up I was constantly referred to as Shola's brother and that frustrated me because at the time I wanted to be recognized for being me, not just someone's brother. So I guess you could say that motivated me even more. Shola was an invaluable help to me during the roller-coaster ride of growing up in football because he'd already been through everything I was going through, so I could trust that his advice came from a place of vast experience. I will always be grateful for his guidance.

Do you and Shola have banter about who is the better player?
Yes, we sometimes joke about it, but honestly you'll have to ask
me that at the end of my career because Shola has spent 13 years
playing in what I believe is the best league and in a World Cup with
Nigeria, which are amazing career achievements. It makes me so
proud and I see him as my inspiration, not my competition.

**Obviously you've been on loan to a couple of clubs. How has
that helped your development?**
I'd say more so my loan at Cardiff City forced me to mature not just
as a player on the pitch but also as a person off it, since it was my
first time living away from home and it was hugely beneficial to me.
Going into a new club as an established player and not just feeling
like a local boy has been good for my self-confidence too. I've also
had the opportunity to play a few different positions on the field,
which has helped with my understanding of the game and my
versatility as a player.

Best player you've ever played against and why?

The first match I ever started for Newcastle was against Manchester
City, and I have to say Yaya Touré was the best player on the pitch
by a country mile – he was so quick and powerful that we couldn't
do anything to stop him.

Best goal you've ever scored?
I'd say my best goal was on my loan debut for Middlesbrough, which
was actually against Cardiff City, who went on to get promoted that
season. I picked up the ball at the side of the penalty box then
shimmied between two defenders and smashed it into the top corner.
I'm pretty proud of that one.

**You've played for Nigeria U20 and England U21. Why did you
end up choosing to represent England?**
I was invited to a training camp in Turkey, followed by a few games
out in Dubai with Nigeria, but other than the delightful weather, I didn't
really enjoy it due to homesickness. So when I was approached by

Sammy Ameobi

England here at home, I couldn't pass up the opportunity and had a couple of memorable years with their U21s. Since growing up, though, I've been drawn back to wanting to represent Nigeria, just as my brother has, and I am eagerly working towards an opportunity to do so.

Sammy, would you mind sharing your testimony with us?
I was brought up in a Christian home. My dad was a pastor, so every Sunday he and mum would drag all the kids to church. I always believed in God but growing up I never really had a personal relationship with him. I guess I just assumed I could be a passive believer until I was old, and then make a commitment. I'd say age 16 to 18 were probably my gloomiest years during my scholarship with Newcastle, where I completely turned away from God. Peer pressure kicked in and my whole lifestyle changed.

Despite all that, God was still faithful, continued blessing me and made a way as I excelled into the Newcastle first team. Even though I'd fulfilled my childhood dream, that wasn't enough for me and I began searching in all the wrong places for a true joy and peace that only comes from God. It wasn't until I was around 21 that I finally decided to turn back and give my life to him, and it's been the best decision I've ever made. I won't lie and say the past couple of years have been all smooth sailing. I still struggle and mess up from time to time, but the reassuring conviction that I am forgiven, that God will always be with me and that I have an eternal future ahead, is more than enough, so I'll never look back.

How does being a Christian change the way you conduct yourself on the field?
Football is such a widely and critically opinionated sport nowadays, even more so with the rise of social media. In the past I would feel so much pressure stepping out on to the field, worrying about what people thought of me, and it would restrict my style of play to the point where I was afraid to make any mistakes. I'd immediately check my Twitter account after every game, hoping for some positive comments, and if they were negative I'd let it ruin my whole week by constantly thinking about it. The thing is, if you live for people's

compliments, you'll die by their criticism, and I learnt this the hard way. I'm not saying there's anything wrong with social media, just the way that I was using it was doing me more harm than good.

Now, as a Christian, I'm at so much more peace that I can play with freedom and a smile on my face because I realize that God gave me this gift, and I'm going to use it to glorify his name fully, knowing that he already loves me and approves of me even if people don't.

Do you think Christian players should be more open about their faith?
Yes, I most definitely do, along with all other Christian athletes. We're on such a visible platform now that I believe we should set good examples and hope to inspire those who are watching. You never know whose lives you may be affecting.

Do you find the fame of being a footballer difficult?
At first I thought it was so amazing that people recognized me but that quickly wore off, and I suddenly went through a period of bitterness towards people – I'd even sometimes be rude when I didn't want to be bothered. Ever since I came back to God the phrase 'blessed to be a blessing' has been lodged in the back of my mind. I realize that he has not lifted me up just for myself but to glorify his name and to make an impact in the lives of others. So now when people approach me, even if I feel like I'm having the worst day, I'll still put on my best smile and be polite because, who knows, maybe that one positive interaction will completely turn someone's day around.

How has football made an impact on your Christian life?
Football has challenged my faith in so many ways – the worries of failure and disappointment can sometimes consume my thoughts and seep out into every area of my life. On the other hand, when things are going well it can lead to self-pride and forgetting to give all honour where it is due, for that which God has done in and through me. One thing I'm learning in this season of my life is how to be content without becoming complacent. There is so much money and materialism involved in and around football nowadays that it becomes

very easy to envy what others have. At the same time, I also don't want to become overly satisfied with what I have accomplished or gained so far, unaware of the potential dangers a mindset like that can have.

Favourite Bible verse?
My favourite verse is Proverbs 3.5–6, 'Trust in the LORD with all your heart and lean not on your own understanding; in all your ways submit to him, and he will make your paths straight.' I love this verse.

What advice would you give to young Christian footballers starting out in their football career?
Another favourite verse of mine is Matthew 6.33–34, 'But seek first his kingdom and his righteousness, and all these things will be given to you as well. Therefore do not worry about tomorrow, for tomorrow will worry about itself. Each day has enough trouble of its own.' All I would say to young Christian footballers is: actively choose to put God first in every area of your life, including football; trust in him because he already knows exactly what you need and has so much in store for you; finally, don't let your worries about tomorrow affect your relationship with God today.

'I believe in God and that he helps you through'

Full name:	**Darren Ashley Bent**
DOB:	6 February 1984
Born:	Tooting, London
Clubs:	Ipswich Town, Charlton Athletic, Tottenham Hotspur, Sunderland, Aston Villa, Fulham (loan), Brighton and Hove Albion (loan), Derby County
Position:	Striker

Andy Clarke Photography

Darren Bent

So Darren, how are you finding life in the Championship?

Yeah, it's not too bad. I mean, years ago I started in the Championship and I was playing regularly for Ipswich Town, and to be fair the football now is a lot better than it was back then. There are now more teams trying to play and it's a really entertaining league. I know there are maybe now people enjoying watching the Championship more than other leagues, because literally anyone can beat anyone, so it's a good and exciting league to play in. I am really, really enjoying it.

Looking back, in your early days you started at Ipswich and Charlton. Is that where you put yourself on the footballing map as a striker?

Yeah, I started at Ipswich Town but was predominantly on the right; then at Charlton I played centre forward and the goals flew in for the two seasons I was there. So that was what got me my move to Tottenham and it was great for me down there. A few things went really well and it is a club that I will always hold in high regard and always give thanks to.

Alan Curbishley was the manager who gave me the opportunity to play in the Premier League. He believed in me and I like to think that I repaid him. He was only there for one season before he left, but I managed to score a lot of goals for him.

As you have already alluded to, Tottenham was a big move, with a transfer fee of around £16.5m. Did you feel the pressure with that fee?

I did, to be fair. When I look back at it now, it was a lot because it was so much money and I'd only played at Charlton and Ipswich, so this was the step up. At the time, when people were asking me, I said that it didn't really faze me, but when I look back now it was quite a tough time. However, it was an experience that I really enjoyed and it's a place that I hold in high regard.

While you were at Spurs, what was it like to be managed by Harry Redknapp? Interesting I suspect?

It was kind of a day-to-day thing where you didn't really know what was going to happen, but to be fair to him, when he came to Tottenham we were really struggling; we needed a lift and he gave everyone that. I think we were nearly rock-bottom when he took over, but he settled everything down and from there things started to go really well.

Let's make the best XI of footballers you have played with.

Goalkeeper – Scott Carson
Right back – Glen Johnson
Centre back – Ledley King
Centre back – Rio Ferdinand
Left back – Ashley Cole
Right centre midfielder – Steven Gerrard
Centre midfielder – Luka Modrić
Left centre midfielder – Danny Murphy
Right attacking midfielder – Ashley Young
Centre forward – Wayne Rooney
Left attacking midfielder – Stewart Downing

So you have been capped 13 times for England, scoring four goals. How proud are you of the achievement?

I am really proud. I like to think with the amount of goals I scored that I would have got more caps and goals but it just wasn't meant to be. You never fully quit playing for England unless you retire, but yes I am really proud of being able to represent my country. I would like to get more caps and you can never say never, but obviously with the crop of attacking young players that we've got at the moment, with Harry Kane, Rooney still there, Sturridge, Welbeck, Vardy, it's tough.

We have quite a rich range of strikers. You never know – I need to get into the Premier League and score a few goals. I still feel that I have a lot to give, and if you can score goals in the Premier League then you can in any division. I managed to do that, so there's no reason why not. I am 31 – it's not like I am 35, I've still got time. If I can stay injury-free and do what I need to do then hopefully in the near future I will be firing again.

We have to ask you about the 'balloon goal' incident against Liverpool back in October 2009. Looking back, do you feel it should have stood?

It's a hard one, because it never came up before that happened and it won't come up again. People said to me that it shouldn't have counted, but there's no doubt when fans throw crisp packets on the pitch. After the event people said to me that it shouldn't have counted and I was, like, 'Well I didn't know that', so maybe it shouldn't have done. At the end of the day, what can I do? It was just one of these freak things that happens. It was quite funny to be part of something like that. Also, to be fair, what people forget about is that we absolutely battered them [Liverpool] that day. People go on about the balloon goal but we deserved to win.

So talking off the pitch: you are open about your faith in God. Has he always been central in your life?

My grandparents have always been quite religious and they were the ones who got me involved. It was from a really young age. Even now they go to church every Sunday. I think my faith is just normal to me now. I read my Psalm book every day, part of the Bible every day, and now it's just become second nature.

The people who are close to me are just used to me doing it and they don't know any different. I believe in God and that he helps you through so many things, but I also have good people around me as well.

As a professional footballer, is it tough to balance living a life that glorifies God with the money, the fame and all of those temptations that come with being who you are?

Not so much really. It's just a case of trying to live a good life anyway. I don't like to be too flamboyant – I like to enjoy nice things but at the same time I like to try and give something back, maturely.

You said in an interview in the past, 'I don't get any stick for my faith in the dressing room.' So with that in mind, have you ever had any positive 'God chats' with the top players you've played with?

Not really, because a lot of them have their own religious beliefs, but to be honest, I also haven't got any jip from any of the guys because it's each to their own. I don't try and push my faith on any other people, just like they wouldn't try and push it on me. If they aren't into it then that's up to them. I don't really judge people one way or the other.

Do you have any Christian football friends you can bounce off and chat with?

I might talk to Kieran Richardson because he's a big believer, but apart from that I don't really like to force it.

Do Sunday matchdays ever annoy you?

It's very rarely an issue, to be honest. Back in the day it might have been but it has become part and parcel of my time now; it's just become second nature.

12

'When you are willing to work hard and pray, anything is possible'

Full name: **Kwadwo Asamoah**
DOB: 9 December 1988
Born: Kumasi, Ashanti, Ghana
Clubs: Udinese, Juventus
Position: Midfielder

Kwadwo Asamoah

Kwadwo, who was your football idol growing up?
Andrea Pirlo was one of my favourites and it was great for me as a
player because I had an opportunity to play with him for three years. I
can say this is something great for me, it is not only about his football.
When he was here I saw him outside of football, his personality, his
way of talking to people; he is a very nice person and very humble.
When you talk about Andrea there are a lot of people who know that
he is a very good player, but if you get close to him then you know
that he is a different person.

**So you played your football as a young man in Ghana. Did you
believe that one day you would make the step-up?**
Yes, I used to tell my younger brother, when he used to watch the
Champions League on TV, that in five years' time he would see me
playing on there. It was just a dream, I was just saying it, and within
four years I was in Europe. It was something that I was thinking of
doing and by God's grace it came true.

**So you got your big move, first to Udinese, but then what was it
like to join Italian giants Juventus? How did it come about?**
It didn't just happen like that. I took a step before getting here and it
wasn't easy. For you to be a part of this team and to even play is not
easy, because you can see the great players we have and it all comes
down to hard work. I started from somewhere and it was all about
hard work and prayers. When you are willing to work hard and pray,
anything is possible.

What would you say is the best thing about living in Italy?
I have been here for almost eight years now and I am more
comfortable because I am used to the lifestyle, so I can say that
the culture is great. I cannot say that I have regretted playing in Italy.
You cannot come here without learning the language because when
you go to training you talk to everyone – even the coach is going
to speak Italian.

What's been your highlight so far, from your time in a Juventus shirt?

Here in Italy we have a lot of great teams, like Milan and Inter, Napoli and Roma. We also play in the Champions League against some of the top teams in the world. I have played in a lot of important games for this team.

You are now an experienced player at international level as well. What's it like to have played in two World Cups and the African Cup of Nations?

It is just great because it is a dream for every player to play for his country and also to play in the World Cup. For a country to qualify for the World Cup, it is not easy, it comes with joy, and even being a part of it is not an opportunity that every player gets. Being with the team twice at a World Cup is great for me and also I have played at three or four of the African Cup of Nations, so I really appreciate what God has helped me do in my career.

Who is the best player you've ever played with?

In my team I have played against a lot of great players, and even before coming here I played for Udinese and we had a captain – Di Natalie. He was an amazing player. When it comes to Juventus, it's difficult because I have played with so many greats, you can't just mention one. It is a great achievement for me. Not every African player gets to play with these great players and in this great team. I am so grateful for that.

So let's reverse that: best player you have played against?

I can mention a few who it wasn't easy playing against because of their speed and their skill. I managed to do what I could against the likes of Cristiano Ronaldo, Juan Cuadrado and Gareth Bale – those are the three. It wasn't easy playing against them.

Let's talk about your faith now, Kwadwo. Where did your love for God come from?

I was brought up in a Christian home because my dad and my mum are both Christians, so I started when I was young. My dad used to teach us about the word of God and we would go to church every Sunday. That is when I started to get to know God and his word.

Do you have fellow Christian players you meet with to talk about your relationship with God?

At Juventus, I do not know, but in my national team there are a few who are Christians. We all know that we worship and believe in one God, we talk about the word of God and encourage each other.

Does God feature in your matchday routine? In what way?

I pray before leaving the hotel – I make sure that I pray before I leave. Then before the start of the game, I pray as well. After the game, when I get home I have to pray, because sometimes you will be happy but sometimes you will be sad after the team has lost. Either way, when I get home or when I am about to go to bed, I will thank God for everything.

Do you have any idea what God has in store for you in the years to come?

I believe in the word of God and I know that it is not my strength or my ability, it is the word of God that has really helped me. Even outside of football it is the way that I carry myself. I respect everyone because of the way that I was brought up. Also, sometimes in football we need luck, and in all of this luck there is God doing all of these things in my career.

I cannot say that it is my talent that is pushing me because I know some people in Ghana who are more talented than me. But because I have the favour of God I am in a good position now. I am playing in a big team and not everybody has that opportunity. I can say that where I am now is down to God, and he has given me the favour to be here.

What advice would you give to other Christian footballers in the game?

What I would say to others to advise them is that football is not something easy – it comes with a lot of things. It takes determination, hard work and prayers. A lot of players started but couldn't finish because they didn't believe and they just gave up. So in everything they do, they should just know there is God and just believe in their own ability.

We all come and have different talents. Maybe there are some things I can do that other people cannot do. Some can do what I cannot do, so each and everyone just needs to know that there is someone up there that can help. I think that if you believe then you can do anything, no matter how difficult it is. In your career you sometimes go through difficult times and you have to be strong. It is not easy but I believe. You cannot say that everything in life will be so perfect for you. At times it will be a bit difficult, and that's when you have to believe that you can do it. It is not the end.

'All honour and glory to him'

Full name: **Leandro Castán da Silva**
DOB: 5 November 1986
Born: Jaú, São Paulo, Brazil
Clubs: Atlético Mineiro, Helsingborg, Barueri, Corinthians, AS Roma
Position: Defender

Leandro Castán

What was football like growing up in Brazil?
I grew up watching my dad play football because he was also a professional footballer; I used to watch him from the side of the pitch. That's why I fell in love with the game. I used to play in the streets of Brazil where I lived, and that was one of the best times of my life.

Who did you always admire as a younger player and why?
I've always admired the Brazilian Ronaldo because he was simply the best player I had ever seen. I then had the privilege of playing alongside him during the end of his career.

What's been your career highlight?
For me, I have two highlights that are just unforgettable. The first has to be winning the Libertadores Cup with Corinthians. The second is representing my country, Brazil, at international level.

How are you enjoying your time at Roma?
I'm enjoying it very much. I'm trying really hard to come back to the professional game after a serious illness. In terms of my personal life, I guess you could say I'm not doing so great, but in terms of my spiritual life I'm doing really well with God. Also, I've been working with a pastor here called Rodrigo Zuliane, and together we have planted a new evangelical church in Rome, which is great.

Best player you've ever played with?
For me, it has to be the Brazilian Ronaldo. With everything that has happened in his career and then coming back even better, he is just a phenomenon. He is a true example of a brilliant player.

Who is the best striker you've ever had to play against and why?
Lionel Messi. It is just impossible to get the ball off of him, he is just unbelievable.

If you could play alongside any centre back in the world, past or present, who would it be and why?
I would love to play alongside my brother, Luciano Castán, who plays for São Bernardo in Brazil. That is a dream that I would love to fulfil one day.

You have played for Brazil twice. How much does this mean to you?
It's a huge achievement for me, the height of my playing career so far. Even though I have only played for Brazil a few times, there is incredible emotion in putting on the Brazil shirt. For those players who have already worn the jersey, they know how much it means to us as players to wear it and represent our country. It will be a dream to one day play for them again.

How did you become a Christian?
My parents became Christians in 1994. I was just eight years old at the time. I grew up in church from a young age and it's always been a part of my life. I was then baptized in 1998 and now I just cannot see my life without Jesus.

How does your faith have an impact on your football career?
My faith is the base of everything in my life thanks to God. I have to give all honour and glory to him. I have merely been chosen by God to be where I am today and I am just so thankful to him for that.

Do you connect with any other Christian players?
Not really, I don't have lots of Christian friends in football. However, when I play against another team or I see a few guys at an event outside of football, we will always have a chat about our faith together.

What has God been teaching you recently?
He has definitely been teaching me that everything depends on him. We need to rely on God, because without him we are nothing.

Do you think football can help bring others to know Christ?
Yes, absolutely. I even have an example of this. I host a service round my house where people can come round to talk about God, and we also have the opportunity to pray together. Football has given me this opportunity to reach out to other people in this way.

How do you deal with the pressures of football?
I just try to remain calm and remember that God is with me. Even though there are things that can tempt us in life and be bad for us, I try my best to live a life that is an example to others.

'Always put God first'

Full name:	**Saido Berahino**
DOB:	4 August 1993
Born:	Bujumbura, Burundi
Clubs:	West Bromwich Albion, Northampton Town (loan), Brentford (loan), Peterborough United (loan)
Position:	Striker

Saido Berahino

Who was your footballing role model when you were growing up?
Zinedine Zidane. I fell in love with him watching the 1998 World Cup back in Africa and I just adored him as a footballer. I remember his two headers in the final and I've still got a picture of myself wearing the French shirt from back then. What a footballer – it was a pity how his French career ended in the 2006 World Cup but he was still named Player of the Tournament despite that sending off in the final. I haven't liked Italy ever since!

Were you surprised when West Brom came in for you at the age of 11? How did it come about?
To be honest, I didn't really know what it was all about when they came in for me. I had only been in the country a year and when Steve Hopcroft [West Brom's Head of Academy Recruitment] invited me on trial I had no knowledge of what was to come. But it was great for me in all sorts of ways – my English really started to improve and I began to enjoy my football with the academy. I was living in Aston just a short distance from the Villa ground at the time but I had never been to a Premier League game. I remember my first big match was at the Hawthorns when I was about 12 and went to see Albion v. Spurs which Spurs won 1–0. A penalty I think.

What's the best thing about being a pro footballer?
The best thing? That's easy – doing something that you love to do day in, day out, and it's never the same. It's not like an office job where you might have a routine. In football, it's like every day something different is there to challenge you. Really, you should challenge yourself every day. Sometimes you are flying, sometimes you go through tough weeks. You just never know because you can go to a game feeling great and expecting to play well and play badly, while at the same time you go into a game not feeling at your best and you play well. But every game is a thrill for me. I am lucky, I know I am, to have this as my job.

As a Manchester United 'supporter', what was it like scoring against them in the Premier League?
I've spoken about this before and my answer never changes. I blanked out. Honestly, when I look back at the celebrations I think to myself, 'That isn't me!' It was my first Premier League goal as well. It was only when I got home to watch it on *Match of the Day* that it actually sank in. That's when it dawned on me that I had scored a winning goal against Manchester United at Old Trafford. After the game, Rio Ferdinand gave me his shirt and gave me some advice: 'Keep working hard,' he said.

Who is the best strike partner that you have played with?
Now this is difficult and could get me into a lot of trouble with my teammates! Honestly, I am grateful to everyone I have played alongside; they have all had an influence on me and my game. I suppose, because of his status in the game, I was really grateful to have a few months alongside Nicolas Anelka. I also have to mention the England U21s, I enjoyed playing next to Harry Kane. But really, I appreciate all the teammates.

Best player that you have ever played against?
Oh that's difficult, who do I choose? Jermain Defoe is a great striker and Samuel Eto'o, but I'd probably say Sergio Agüero. He is the complete forward, so clinical, so strong and a nightmare for defenders.

Tell us, what drove you to create the Saido Berahino Foundation?
Well, that all comes from my background, my start in life. Even from my youngest days I always had something at the back of my mind that said to me that if God blessed me in some way, I would try to help the less fortunate around me. It is as simple as that really. I wanted to give kids hope. The Foundation now is focusing on the huge number from my homeland in Burundi who have taken refuge in Rwanda. I am making plans to go to Africa this summer to see the work for myself. My mum went out earlier this year to see things for

herself and my Foundation has supported the building of a school which opens in Gambia this summer and I want to go there for the opening.

Saido, tell us your testimony of how you came to know God?
For me, coming from Africa, loads of people believe in God; God is a place of safety. My family have always had that belief and that drove me to find out who God is, to ask for his protection. But my first real direct experience of feeling this was after I suffered a bad knee injury a few years ago and I went through a very tough, tough period in my life. Only God could have witnessed what I went through and only God could have given me the strength to go through that and turn my life around. From that moment, my faith has become stronger.

How does God feature in your matchday routine?
Massively. The moment I wake up on matchdays I will read a verse from the Bible. No particular verse, something I will just choose and when I go to the game, just before it starts I will pray on the pitch. I cannot play without doing these things. If I score, you will always see me point to the heavens as part of my celebrations. I always look to the heavens thanking God for this blessing.

Are there any fellow footballers or teammates who you share your faith with?
Yes, me and Victor Anichebe will sometimes talk about it but not a lot.

What has God taught you through being a professional footballer?
To be humble – if you humble yourself before God then there are greater things ahead. It's sometimes hard with the positions and situations you find yourself in as a professional footballer but you have to try to not get carried away. Only God can make it possible although obviously you have to make the journey yourself. Recently, I went through a difficult time which has been well publicized when a lot of people were trying to help me but it was going in one ear and out the other. Until I came back to my senses and realized myself where I was going wrong, I couldn't change my path. God doesn't allow you to do

bad things but the devil can get in there and take you down the wrong path and it is God that brings you back. It comes from inside and you pray for forgiveness and direction.

Do you believe that prayer affects performance?
Yes, of course. You don't pray for hat-tricks or great goals – you pray for guidance, for protection, to stay healthy.

What advice would you give to young Christian footballers starting out in their careers?
Always put God first – whatever you do. Live right, eat well, train well, train hard, play and enjoy but always with God in mind.

'God had a bigger plan for my life'

Full name:	**Linvoy Stephen Primus**
DOB:	14 September 1973
Born:	Forest Gate, London
Clubs:	Charlton Athletic, Barnet, Reading, Portsmouth. Retired in 2009
Position:	Defender

Jonny Reid/Christians in Sport

Linvoy Primus

What was it like to be a professional footballer?

My experience was that it was a great time in my life, to do something that I have always dreamt of doing. The challenges that come along with it can make it difficult at times. However, you have good moments and testing moments. When you're in the team and playing well, obviously it's much better; and it's not so great when you're not involved – but generally, being a footballer was really good.

When did you start to play football?

I started playing football when I was 12 years old, for a Sunday team. Two years later, when I was 14, I got scouted for Charlton. Then when I turned 16 they offered me an apprenticeship, and then at 18 I was offered a professional contract.

Linvoy, give us a flavour of what the pressures are like of being a footballer.

I think the pressures are always there you know – trying to play well, trying to win football matches, looking for your next contract. So there is always a certain amount of pressure that comes with football. No matter how good you are, there is always something that you want to achieve, whether that's for yourself or for your club; so the pressures can be quite intense. That's why you see the good players who handle it well and remain at the top; and the ones who are too inconsistent never quite make it.

What would you say was your career highlight?

I have a few. My career highlights for me were probably getting promoted to the Premier League with Portsmouth. Also going on to win the FA Cup with Portsmouth – even though I wasn't part of the team, I was in the squad. Finally, obviously scoring in games was amazing for me being a defender, but to score two goals in a single game was pretty special.

Is being a footballer really as good as it sounds?

That's a really good question. I think everyone has their own experiences. My own experience was that I enjoyed football to a

degree. Did I always love it? No, not always. There's lots of challenges
that you need to overcome, and I think being a footballer always looks
more glamorous from the outside rather than the inside. There's things
that you will just never know about unless you're a footballer, and it's
certainly a job with its ups and downs.

OK then: what's the best thing about being a footballer?
I would say it's being able to do something that I dreamt of doing
since I was a kid. You're able to play football with your teammates,
who end up becoming your friends. There's probably some other bits
and pieces, but when you strip away all the material things, I think it
is just the love of the game and being able to play with your mates.

**Linvoy, as a Christian, how did you combat the pressures of
football?**
Well, one of the biggest things for me was prayer. When going
through certain situations, I'd always turn to what the Bible says
and let that guide me through. So I'd definitely say those two
things: prayer and reading the word of God.

Tell us your testimony.
Well, in 2001 I was invited to church. At that time my wife wasn't
doing too well health-wise, and some guys I knew invited us to
church. I'd never really given church much thought before then, but
when I went I knew there was something missing from my life; there
was an emptiness even though I was doing the thing I loved. So
I listened to the guy talk at the front, and he was sharing about his
relationship with Jesus – that got me asking questions of myself and
of faith. Six weeks after that, and continuing asking those questions to
friends and teammates, I decided that I needed to know who this Jesus
was and have him in my life. So from that day I began a new life,
trying to live a life that God had planned for me as a follower of him.

Is it hard to be a Christian in the world of football?
It is difficult at times because some people just don't understand the
Christian life; and with that, people will have a laugh at you and a dig.

But with those digs at you can come questions. Once people begin to ask questions and ask why you believe in it, they start to understand what it all means. It can be difficult, but it's about trying to be faithful to God and living your life in the right way. Sometimes the jokes would get out of hand and I'd find it really hard to deal with it, but I leant on Scripture and remembered that Jesus was persecuted when he was on this earth. So I kept strong, and after about a year these teammates who were once laughing at me for my faith were now asking for me to pray for them. They saw a change in my life both on and off the field, and that had more of an impact than any amount of words I said could have.

Do you have a favourite Bible verse?
My favourite Bible verse is Jeremiah 29.11, '"For I know the plans I have for you," declares the LORD, "plans to prosper you and not to harm you, plans to give you hope and a future."' When I first became a Christian a young lad sent me a letter with this verse on it. I used to worry about life, and this verse taught me that God had a bigger plan for my life than just being a footballer.

What are you up to now since your retirement from football?
Well, I'm doing a number of things now. I get invited out by schools, prisons and churches to share my faith. I also work for a Christian charity called Christians in Sport (<www.christiansinsport.org.uk>), where I meet with Christian pro footballers up and down the country and also club chaplains. It's great! I love hearing about players' faiths and chatting to them about how their journey with God is going. So I feel like I'm doing the right thing at the moment, and I'm enjoying it too.

'You need to discover him for yourself'

Full name: **Tobi Alabi**
DOB: 5 November 1993
Born: England
Clubs: West Ham United, Millwall, Ljungskile SK, Metropolitan Police. Retired in 2013
Position: Striker

Brian Tonks

Tobi Alabi

Growing up, was it always going to be football for you?
It was: ever since I was young, that is all I remember. It is the cliché story, really, in that it was all I ever wanted to do since I was a kid. I was always out in the streets playing football; I was always pestering my parents to get me a new football, and playing with my older brother, and I think that really helped me. I played with him and his friends from about five or six onwards, so it helped me a lot.

Who was your footballing hero back then?
Thierry Henry, without a shadow of a doubt. He was king and obviously, as an Arsenal fan, he is someone I have always looked up to. You know, when you think you are going to be that player but you never are, you just admire them from a distance.

As a youngster you were snapped up by West Ham and then came through the ranks at Millwall – both big clubs. How did this come about?
Yes, I started at West Ham (and thankfully not many of the Millwall fans know that); so I started out there when I was seven, but they didn't actually sign me properly into the academy. They had me in for training and some matches but I was still playing for my Sunday team as well. Then a year later Millwall came in and offered me something solid, so I took it. At the time I didn't really understand the rivalry; I was just thinking that an academy wants me and so I was buzzing.

Millwall actually taught me a lot, but when I was young I didn't really realize the impact of me being there until I was about 13 years old – at which time the guy who had scouted me told my dad that I was one of the boys they were looking to release. This came as a bit of a reality check for me because as a footballer you end up being idolized in your area, and so I was slacking in training. That was something I had to come to terms with very quickly and deal with because I was given six months to turn it around. It was a pride hit because I was thinking that if I get released, who am I?

Then my dad worked with me in the garden and it got to the stage in secondary school where every day after school I used to go and play by myself. That really instilled that work ethic in me that I carried through to today, so it was a big turning point in my life.

What were your ambitions at that point, being early on in your career?
Well I didn't actually end up getting released because I turned it around and they extended my contract. It's funny how things work because a year later, after all of that work I had put in, Arsenal and Reading actually came in with bids to buy me from Millwall. I think a lot of the things that you go through mould you, and that was another point in my life that moulded me. To believe that hard work pays off, it is so cliché but at the same time it is so true. So in 24 months I had gone from being told that I may well be released, to Arsenal bidding for me, plus during that time they were winning things as well, so they were a big club.

At the end of the day Millwall ended up rejecting all of those offers and gave me a four-year contract. I was buzzing, and that was when I knew that all I needed to do was to work hard – it wasn't rocket science. I was really happy and it gave me real focus and a drive to get into that first team and progress. The ambition was still to play in the Premier League and to play for Arsenal, despite just signing a new contract at Millwall.

Tell us some of your testimony and how you encountered God.
My parents are actually pastors, so I have grown up in the church from birth. Yes, it is a good start, but that comes with its challenges because it is something that I didn't discover myself, it is something that I was born into. It is funny because everyone has their own challenges; to have a relationship with God you need to discover him for yourself and you need to understand why you are doing it. I feel, like, being in a church so young, I didn't actually know why I was doing it, until I was older; and I didn't really know why I should serve God. It was the right thing to do because my parents went to church, but I think with everything I have experienced, it is only now that I

understand and have grown in my relationship with him. So in essence, it is only really in the last three years that my relationship with God has begun to grow properly.

How has God used those tough times in your life to strengthen you, with your heart condition and having to retire from football at 19?

You know what: it's crazy. I want to give you proper answers and there are so many different components. After the whole ordeal and speaking to people who have similarly to me been close to death, it's like after that happens, you go through stages. The first is confusion, the second is anger and the third stage is usually where you become a philosopher, wondering about what the purpose of life is, is God real and what happens after? All of those things start coming into play, and I spent a long time after the incident thinking, 'What is the purpose of what we are doing?'

In terms of recovering, I didn't really deal with it head on. The way I dealt with it was to throw myself into the campaign [Heart4More] initially. I really spent a lot of time saying to myself that there needs to be a purpose in my life and I need to do something long lasting. All the things you do as a football player – money, cars, clothes and girls – you don't take these with you. So for me, when we are on earth you need to have impact and do something beneficial for someone else. I feel like God has brought me through everything I have been through to prepare me for what I am doing now, and if I didn't play football then I wouldn't have the platform to do that. I feel like it was all preparation for what is to come.

How soon after your recovery did you decide to set up the Heart4More Foundation?

The Heart4More Foundation was actually never meant to be a foundation, it was just simply the angry 19-year-old who needed to vent his frustrations somehow and to raise awareness. So that's all I wanted to do, and through that I had to do some publicity events and even went into my old school to talk about the heart and cardiac arrest. Doing this hit me because I was going out to talk to these children – I could inspire them for a day but other than that, what was I putting in place for them?

After that I sat down with one of my friends and I had been getting pestered to make a charity for a long time but I never wanted to do it. I said that I didn't want to do that but it came to light that putting something in place to serve young people was the only way for me to fulfil my idea of longevity. So that was how I came to the decision of launching a foundation. The next thing was, 'What is the name of the foundation going to be?' So while I was in hospital, two days after my operation, Toby Porter, the mouthpiece for Millwall, interviewed me, and the headline was, 'Young Lion Has Heart For More'. So I said, 'What about Heart4More?'

What is your dream for the foundation, that motivates you?
When I was talking to these people at school and asking them what they want to do, they would say: 'Bricklayer' or 'I will work at my dad's plumbing firm' or 'I will work in retail'. However, when I spoke to them on their own they were coming out with things like 'An investment banker' or 'A petroleum engineer', and so I asked, 'Why didn't you say that in front of these people?' After that, one of the first things I realized that we needed to tackle is the aspirational levels of young people. Too many think they are only going to be a product of their environment or what their family have achieved. Cardiac awareness is always going to be the key focus of the foundation, but now my drive and passion is for youth. We are trying to become a stronger force for young people to rely on and to help them progress.

How excited are you about what God has in store for Heart4More?
I am so excited, honestly. I am so excited because I feel like I have come into my own and the drive is there, the ambition is there. I really feel that God is connecting me to the right people. So I just can't wait to see what he has in store for us in the next five to ten years.

'Put the word of Christ in first place'

Full name:	**Anderson Hernanes de Carvalho Viana Lima**
DOB:	29 May 1985
Born:	Recife, Brazil
Clubs:	São Paulo, Santo Andre (loan), Lazio, Inter Milan, Juventus
Position:	Midfielder

Hernanes

First, who was your football idol, growing up in Brazil as a young boy?
I would probably say Felipe Jorge, but I can't say that he was my idol in that sense.

How did you get scouted for São Paulo academy at such a young age? What was the story behind it?
In January 2001, when I was 15 years old, I left my home town of Recife and went to São Paulo to have trials at some of the bigger teams in the city. I went with three friends and with the father of two of them; we stayed together in that time. I remember that it was around September of the same year and I had already been through many trials at some of the clubs, but none of them had successfully scouted me. Then in October an opportunity appeared for me to go to São Paulo's academy. I had so much determination to join the club and thanks to God, I finally got signed by São Paulo.

Did you always think you were going to make it as a professional footballer?
My life has always been about football. I've always been with the ball at my feet, playing alone or with friends. But I would say when I turned 17 years old and I was in the São Paulo academy, that's when I decided to give my everything to make it as a professional.

Jumping forward now: was it a hard decision to leave Brazil for Serie A in Italy?
No, not for me because I wanted to wait for the right time to leave Brazil and I was prepared to do that when the offer came in from Lazio.

Would you say your time at Lazio is where you got yourself noticed on the world stage?
I think so. There was quite a prestigious magazine that I was featured in when I was playing for São Paulo in Brazil, but I think it was when I was in Lazio that my name came out.

What was it like to move to two massive clubs like Inter Milan and then Juventus? Did you feel the pressure?

As players, we always know about the pressure that comes with playing for such massive clubs like Inter Milan and Juventus, but I think I only feel it when things aren't going in the right direction.

What's the best thing about being a professional footballer?

For me, it has to be the sensation of scoring a winning goal. To ultimately be paid to do that and allow the fans to feel the same emotions that we have is amazing.

When you are not training or playing, what do you do in your spare time?

I like spending time with family and friends. I often will go to restaurants with my wife and friends and take the children to the cinema.

Who's the best player you've played with?

It has to be Ronaldinho because of his great technique and vision on the pitch. He has a great pass on him and has scored some amazing goals.

You have also featured heavily for the Brazilian national team. How proud are you to have played in the 2014 World Cup?

I can't even comprehend how much it means to me. There is no measure! It was one of my biggest achievements in football.

Let's now talk about your faith, which you are very open about. Tell us about how you first encountered Jesus.

Back in 2001, when I was searching for a club in São Paulo, I stayed some months in a place called Juventus – it is a neighbour of São Paulo. During that time a friend called me to visit his church and I went along. It was that day that I accepted Jesus Christ as my Lord and Saviour.

Have you found it difficult to balance the public football lifestyle with a life that is honouring to God?
No, but I would say that it is not simple. However, I'm in no different position than any other Christian around the world. I always say that everyone is included in the Parable of the Sower that Jesus told. All kinds of people have their problems and obstacles that will try and block their faith, but when you really want to honour God, you find a way.

Do you see yourself as a role model for other Christian footballers?
Yes I do. After ten years of playing for big and important clubs around the world, people have been able to see who I am. Ever since I started, I have always declared my faith in Christ very openly. I try to share the gospel of Jesus as much as I can and in doing that am a role model for young Christian players.

What advice would you give to Christian footballers around the world who are just starting out in their careers?
I would say, put the word of Christ in first place. Read the Bible every day or at least as often as you can, and make a true effort with all your heart to practise what you are reading.

'It is only God that matters'

Full name:	**Victor Chinedu Anichebe**
DOB:	23 April 1988
Born:	Lagos, Nigeria
Clubs:	Everton, West Bromwich Albion
Position:	Striker

West Bromwich Albion FC

Victor Anichebe

Growing up, was it always going to be football for you? Or were there other opportunities?

Well, when I was growing up I wasn't really into football like the rest of the kids. My family were African so they were always on to me about how important school was. Football just came on to me. My friend's dad had a football team, which I went along to, and I was really good on the first day. So I carried that on and it just went from there. I played some Sunday league and then for my district and even got scouted by Crewe Alexandra and Everton. At the time Crewe had an amazing centre of excellence and Everton was a bit daunting, so I went to Crewe.

However, it started affecting my studies because I would get back so late in the evenings. At this point I went over to Everton and broke through. David Moyes and Andy Holden were big mentors for me, so I never went out on loan – the manager wanted to keep me in and around the first team and I benefited from that. I started training in and around the first team around the age of 15–16 and made my debut at 17.

What was David Moyes like as a manager? Do you owe a lot to him?

I would say so. Obviously you owe it to yourself, your family and God, but I would definitely like to play under him again – he was a big help to me. Andy Holden also deserves a mention too as he helped me a lot. They were both great for me and so was James Vaughan – seeing him break through pushed me on to believe I could get through too.

Was it a difficult decision to make the switch to West Bromwich Albion?

Yes it was, it was really difficult, but sometimes when you are in a place for so long you begin to take it for granted. That's normal with everyone, plus I wanted to experience new places, so I made the switch. I felt that it was the right time to go and I had just had one of my better seasons, so I wasn't leaving on a low. If Moyes had still been there then I probably wouldn't have left, but these things happen. It's still something I ask myself now, whether it was the right decision, but this is life sometimes.

What is the best goal you've ever scored?

It would probably be for Everton, when we were in the Europa League. I scored against Nuremburg and won a penalty in that game as well. That goal stands out for me because of how much the fans loved it, and it was just a great journey that we were on as a team that year. I scored plenty of goals in that competition and we were doing really well. Even today people still stop me and ask me if I remember Nuremburg.

Who is the best strike partner you've ever played with?

Oh, James Vaughan, obviously. We had been coming through together since we were under elevens, and without that partnership maybe we wouldn't have even made it. We always used to help each other and we even called ourselves Yorke and Cole at that time. He was probably the best; he was more of the goal-scorer and I set him up. I have played with a lot of good players but he was probably the best.

Who is the best player you've ever played against?

Well, when Nigeria went to the Olympics, we won a silver medal and we played against Argentina, who had everybody playing. They had Sergio Agüero, Ángel Di María, Juan Román Riquelme. They had so many greats and obviously they had Lionel Messi as well, and he was clearly the best. However, Di María was better than him on the day. Where I was playing they still had Ezequiel Garay, at the back, so their team was unbelievable. But despite losing 1–0 it was a great experience. Playing in the Olympics was surreal because it was more than just a match, it is an event. In the Olympic village you see people from all the different sports, all together in one place – tennis players, volleyball players and even Usain Bolt walking around. It was a real community. That silver medal is something that I can look back on in later life as a proud moment, representing my country at a great event.

117

You have represented the Nigerian national team. How proud are you of this achievement?

Yes, it was a hugely proud moment, obviously. I didn't grow up in Nigeria because my dad moved us over here when I was one or two, but I appreciate the life that England has given us. It has given us such a great base, but when you play for your country you are so proud. When you go back you see the way that people adore and love you; it's an amazing feeling. Moyes pushed me to play for England but I wasn't born in England and every single holiday was always spent in Nigeria, so it made more sense for me.

Let's talk about your faith in God. Where did this start for you?

Well, Nigerians are very religious – when you go there you see every bus or bicycle has something about how good God is on it. Whether you are a Muslim or a Christian, faith is very evident over there. My family are all religious so they are the ones who took me to church every Sunday, and that is where it started. When I was younger it was kind of boring: in England it is more sit down and quiet; whereas African church is more singing and dancing. They are just different and both of them serve the same purpose, so I try to go to both. So from my family taking me from a young age, I then went to a Catholic school and it carried on from there. I have been quite an independent person from about the age of 14, so I wanted to go for myself, and in football you can get caught up with all the hype and distractions. I just think God has a plan for us: you can alter the path you take and there might be all kinds of trials and tribulations, but the destination remains the same.

How difficult is it to balance the luxurious football lifestyle with trying to live for God?

I don't think it is difficult because personally I know what I want for my life. I know for other people it might be difficult but for me, I know that football in the grand scheme of things is just a small stepping stone. A lot of people live for football and we are very blessed that God has given us this opportunity, but there are times when people think they are untouchable. They don't give the glory back to God. I just think it depends on what you see life as: many players think that football is the best thing that is ever going to happen to them, but it's really not. It is such a small part of our lives: money comes and goes; fame comes and goes. If you look at Manny Pacquiao, he quoted that when you have Jesus in your life, nothing in this world matters, and that's how I feel.

Have you had any positive conversations about your faith with teammates?

I don't know if you would deem it was positive. You know, a lot of people think that they are open but they are actually really closed off. That is never a problem for me – I would never try to force anyone to believe, but I always just try to question them. I ask them if they do not believe, why that is, why they don't believe. Recently as a team we were away in Austria. We were standing on a cliff looking over and I said to some of the players, 'So you don't believe,' and they didn't really know how to answer. There have been some good conversations but it is really hard because people blame God for bad things that happen in the world. I don't know how to answer these things but at the same time there are many people getting saved and miracles are happening. To them it is luck or down to doctors; I think people need to start looking at the positive side because by the end of our conversations they are unsure, which gets them thinking.

I have also told them about a personal story. Basically it was just when I had moved to West Brom, and one day after training I was driving down the motorway and I was so tired. Ahead there was a bit of traffic and I came off the motorway on to a country lane and I just felt myself completely go to sleep. All I heard was the clearest voice that I have ever heard in my life, and it was shouting my Nigerian name, telling me to wake up, and I couldn't understand. From nowhere I just woke up and found myself on the other side of the road with a lorry coming towards me. I managed to swerve on to the other side of the road. That would have been me gone, absolutely gone.

Something inside me told me to wake up and that was what saved me. I got on the side of the road and was crying, praying and thanking God. Now nobody can test my faith; this has been

19

the clearest thing for me. So when I tell people this, some believe. Nobody can sway me. I feel that these things happen in many people's lives but they don't believe the blessing that happened to them because they have closed minds.

What advice would you give to other Christian footballers who are maybe starting out in their career?

I would say that you have to work hard. You can pray as much as you want but if you don't work hard for yourself then God is not going to give it to you. All the times that you do pray, when you do finally get that opportunity, always give thanks, no matter how good or bad. If you do not give thanks then things can easily get taken away from you. That is the most important thing: when you know that it is only God that matters then everything in life becomes a lot clearer.

Any idea what God has planned for you in the future?

I wouldn't say so. He has a plan for me and I am just here, serving. Whatever comes comes and that is just how I am. My long-term goal is to help people. I aim for those small steps of improvement; hopefully I can improve inside and outside of football.

'Thanks to God, my life is so different now'

Full name:	**Heurelho da Silva Gomes**
DOB:	15 February 1981
Born:	João Pinheiro, Brazil
Clubs:	Cruzeiro, PSV Eindhoven, Tottenham Hotspur, 1899 Hoffenheim (loan), Watford
Position:	Goalkeeper

Heurelho
Gomes

Heurelho Gomes

Growing up in Brazil, what were your earliest memories of playing football?

It was a difficult life to begin with, but of course everything that happened over there makes me stronger and a better person today. It wasn't easy when I was young. I used to live on a farm and I came from a poor family. However, I thank God that I'm now here in England, playing football in the best league in the world.

Did you always want to be a keeper?

No, I never wanted to be a keeper. In Brazil our preference is always about being a striker. I tried to play as a striker, but it didn't quite work out for me and so I ended up playing in goal instead.

What was it like playing in Brazil and being regarded as one of the best keepers around, and then making your way into the Premier League?

Yeah, of course it was nice, but Brazil is very different compared with England. I felt it was an easier league over there but now I'm here it's a lot more technical to be a Premier League goalkeeper. I started to play in goal quite late; I was about 18 years old when I decided to be a keeper, so for me it's a huge achievement to now be a goalkeeper in the best league in the world.

So during your time with Spurs and Watford, what's been your highlight in England?

My focus is never really on a highlight. I don't really like to think about that. My focus is about helping my team, now. I'm not really one for the spotlight. I'm quite quiet and I like to do my talking on the pitch. I never look for my highlight or my best moment. I always want to do the best I can, and this moment now, at this time at Watford, is so special.

How do you deal with the pressures of football?

I can't do this by myself. I have a faith that helps me. Sometimes it's so difficult to deal with the pressures in football, it makes players go crazy. From my position, if a striker doesn't score a goal for one or two games, it's fine. If a goalkeeper makes a mistake, it's fine. For me, God is the most important thing to deal with the pressures like this. For example, my time at Tottenham, I had days where I didn't feel good, but my faith helped me deal with situations over there. Every day I try to do my best because I put God first – that's how I can deal with any kind of pressure.

Best player you've ever played with and why?
Oh, this is a difficult question. There's the Brazilian Ronaldo, you know; he was just incredible. I can mention so many players who I had the pleasure of playing with. Ronaldinho as well. There's Gareth Bale and Luka Modrić. It's so hard – I can name you two teams' worth of amazing players!

So tell us: what's the secret behind your infamous long throw?
My secret! It's natural! To be honest with you, I used to be able to throw it longer than I can now, but it starts to hurt my shoulder a little bit. It's a natural throw for me. It's more technique than power, and I really feel that my throw is better than my kick because I can reach the target more accurately. I remember at the beginning of the 2015/2016 season for Watford, we scored in one of the first games from one of my long throws, and that's good. When I was playing for Cruzeiro, in Brazil, we had this tactic in a game where the Number 10 would come and receive the ball at his feet from my long throw. The attackers would go on to score lots and lots of goals that season because of the throw tactic.

How did you become a Christian?
I came to faith because I believe that you're never going to take anything from here, on this earth, to the tent. I was missing something in my life before I was a Christian, so I started going to church and I began to follow God. Even as a footballer, you need something. Before I met God, I started going a little crazy because everything is there for you when you are a footballer. You have to have something different to take you away from these things, and that's what God did. He took me away from them. I do not need to go out and go to a

nightclub now; I have a family and I'm able to do things better. That's why I changed my life for ever. Before, the things in this world were the best for me; but now, my main target is to do things right for God. Thanks to God, my life is so different now and I'm far happier.

Obviously playing professional football means you're very busy. How do you manage to maintain a closeness to Jesus?

Every Saturday I normally go to church. Obviously, some Saturdays when we are playing an away match, it's difficult to get back in time, but even if I go for just 25 minutes, it's enough. If, after the game, some of the lads say there's a party going on, I tell them, 'OK, enjoy your party, but I am off to church.' Midweek, on a Wednesday, I often go to church too. When I was at Tottenham and things weren't going right for me there, I used to wake up at five o'clock in the morning, travel into London for one hour and go to church to have some time. I think we have to do things like this; God gave us everything and getting up early to spend time with him is nothing in comparison. I know that if I put God in first place then he is faithful. He will never let me down. Everything that I do is not for me, it is for him.

Do you meet up with other Christian footballers?

Sometimes. I normally meet up with David Luiz, especially during international duty with Brazil. I remember during the World Cup, that was really good because we had a pastor over there and it was me, Kaká and Lúcio praying together. Even here in England there are a few players who I can meet up with at times.

Can you give fans an idea of what it's like to be a Christian and a footballer?

You have to be different. You have to show people that there is something different in your life. When you follow Jesus, people can see there's something different about you. It's not going to be easy because not everyone will share your faith, but you have to try to do your best and show people they can have it too. It's not easy, but I have never denied Jesus. People might say that because I am a footballer, I cannot be a Christian because there are so many temptations that come to you. As a footballer who is a Christian, I feel like I should try and be an example to others and show that I am different.

Do you think Christian footballers should be more open about their faith and why?
Yes, I believe so. We need to show what we believe and what is the right thing to do. I believe we as footballers have the power to show who Jesus is and help change people. The power of football is so strong and that's why I upload a picture to Instagram. I will always post a comment about God because all the glory has to go to him. I believe that I need to show people my faith more, so I can help them live life in the right way. I'm not going to force people to change their minds; I'm just here to help them find their way.

Did you know that SPCK is a registered charity?

As well as publishing great books by leading Christian authors, we also . . .

. . . **make assemblies meaningful and fun for over a million children** by running www.assemblies.org.uk, a popular website that provides free assembly scripts for teachers. For many children, school assembly is the only contact they have with Christian faith and culture, and the only time in their week for spiritual reflection.

. . . **help prisoners to become confident readers** with our easy-to-read stories. Poor literacy is a huge barrier to rehabilitation. Prisoners identify with the believable heroes of our gritty fiction. At the same time, questions at the end of each chapter help them to examine their choices from a moral perspective and to build their reading confidence.

. . . **support student ministers overseas in their training** through partnerships in the Global South.

Please support these great schemes: visit www.spck.org.uk/support-us to find out more.